The Contemplation
of Otherness:
The Critical Vision
of Religion

The Contemplation of Otherness: The Critical Vision of Religion

by
Richard Eugene Wentz

MERCER

ISBN 0-86554-135-3

Library of Congress Cataloging in Publication Data:

Wentz, Richard E.
    The contemplation of otherness.

    Includes bibliographical references and index.
    1. Religion—Study and teaching. I. Title.
BL41.W46 1984   207   84-1066
ISBN 0-86554-135-3 (alk. paper)

Contents

Dedication

For Yvonne
Selena, Susanna, Melissa
from whom, for whom
love issues
in the contemplation of otherness

I / The Rage
Against Otherness

Call me Ishmael. Some years ago—never mind how long precisely—having little or no money in my purse, and nothing particular to interest me on shore, I thought I would sail about a little and see the watery part of the world. It is a way I have of driving off the spleen and regulating the circulation. . . . But wherefore it was that after having repeatedly smelt the sea as a merchant sailor, I should now take it into my head to go on a whaling voyage; this the invisible police officer of the Fates . . . can better answer than anyone else. . . . Yet now that I recall all the circumstances, I think I can see a little into the springs and motives which being cunningly presented to me under various disguises, induced me to set about performing the part I did, besides cajoling me into the delusion that it was a choice resulting from my own unbiased free will and discriminating judgement.

Chief among these motives was the overwhelming idea of the great whale himself. Such a portentous and mysterious monster roused all my curiosity. Then the wild and distant seas where he rolled his island bulk; the undeliverable, nameless perils of the whale; these, with all the attending marvels of a thousand Patagonian sights and sounds, helped to sway me to my wish.[1]

So begins the American classic, Moby Dick. *It is the story of Ishmael.* Moby Dick *is* his *book. He begins the story, and he survives to tell it.*

---

[1]Herman Melville, *Moby Dick* (New York: Modern Library, 1950) 1, 5, 6.

*"Call me Ishmael," he says. He is the namesake of a biblical wanderer—
a wanderer because he is a wonderer. He wonders at this world, its
teeming people, all colors, all sizes. He wonders at the gods he has
seen—marvelous gods, who have sent him to his knees, made him run
in terror, and then caused him to dance in ecstasy, sometimes to roll in
the grass in uncontrollable laughter. Such gods! But he has also known
peace as he watched the great whales in their schools, purring and nuz-
zling about the boats like giant kittens, loving and being loved. Ishmael
has stared for hours into the untroubled depths. "Deep down," he ponders, "there I still bathe in the eternal mildness of joy." Some shrouded
other broods there over the watery manger of the whales. Ishmael
knows it.*

 *Ahab? Ahab has gone with his quest. No, not a quest; it was a con-
quest he pursued. Ahab has killed himself in some grand delusion that
aroused a rage against otherness. Moby Dick may be encountered, but
never conquered. There is no harpoon that can finally and ultimately
tear out the heart of the great mystery. Ahab is gone, slain by obsession
and presumption, misunderstanding—dragged into the depths by the
wounded whale. Ahab was no longer human. He was the skeleton of his
own pride, trying to pierce the mask of the white mystery, no longer
aware of anything or anyone. His madness and vengeful fury were all
that were left as he was dragged to death with the Pequod as his coffin.
How Ishmael managed to survive, he does not know. It is a wonder
among all the other wonders he has known. Perhaps it was because
there was in him no rage against otherness.*

  The study of religion is an enterprise very much like the
story of Moby Dick. As one observes the state of the art, the images of
Ishmael and Ahab establish themselves as prominent figures. They
represent two types of approach to religious studies; but Ahab has
been in the ascendancy for some time. Ishmael is a *wonderer*, who
learns many things about the mystery of otherness by way of a simple
mode of detached participation. Ahab is a *stalker*, a possessor, a con-
queror—one who rages against otherness. But Ahab also learns. He
learns by charting the path of his quarry, by observing its ways, its
diet, by becoming a master of the habitat. Ahab knows much about the
ways, the paths, the habitat; but he does not know the other whom he
seeks. The other cannot be known by conquest; and it is not safe to

assume, as Ahab does, that knowing so much of the details, the context, the behavior, makes one a master of the other.

In this chapter it is my purpose to examine the manner in which the study of religion can become a pathological enterprise, like Ahab's pursuit of the white whale. Almost no scholar exists who is not in love with his subject matter. It is safe to assume that the political scientist finds himself committed to the importance of political systems, relationships, and philosophies. No linguist exists who is not fascinated by language. One frequently gets the impression, however, that scholars of religion are either hostile to the substance of their inquiries, or are in mortal fear of having their commitments revealed. They tend to become like Ahab, tormented by the very presence of the "white whale." The mysterious other, Moby Dick, agitates his memory and imagination. He has had a leg torn off in his encounter with the great mystery, and he has decided that it is a monster that must be slain. A fear that perhaps he is dealing with an *other* who is beyond the ordinary, perhaps beyond manipulation, translates itself into rage. He must reduce the mystery so that it becomes like everything else that Ahab controls in the world of ordinary habitation. In conquering the mysterious whale, he would overcome his fear and have his revenge, but only by the destruction of that which gives purpose to his quest. So, in the realm of religious studies, it is a curious matter to observe scholars attempting to slay what they should love.

While a more comprehensive discussion of the character of otherness shall be left to later chapters, it is necessary to clarify the term at this point. There is no existence that is not measured and known by way of encounter with some form of otherness. This fact of otherness gives rise to religion. Our appreciative awareness of the encounter with otherness is the evidence of human religiousness. The total shape of that awareness—expressed in special stories, action, and social formations—may be termed *religion*. Every form of the encounter with otherness is expressive of mystery: there is a sense in which every "other" whom we meet is more than the measure of our meeting.

Religious studies exists in order to gain knowledge and understanding of our religiousness and our religions. Its function is to interpret the multivalent nature of the encounter with otherness. It is possible for some academic disciplines to pretend that no mystery is involved. It is not possible for religious studies to engage in that subterfuge because it is a discipline devoted to *understanding* the mystery. Religious studies should not be fearful of the mystery or hostile toward it—as was Ahab. As a scholar who demonstrates an appreciative awareness of the reality that every other humanistic or scientific enterprise is based upon—the encounter with otherness—the religion scholar should know that learning and truth are received; they are not created ex nihilo by us. Other disciplines may play with the latter assumption, but religious studies should know that it is the mystery of otherness that accounts for everything that exists.

In this regard, the religion scholar is concerned with how our religiousness functions. He should even be able to observe the manner in which scholars tend to be religious about their own enterprises. When the physicist encounters the other in elements of motion, mass, and energy, for example, he devises methods whereby he can examine and even control those characteristics of otherness. If he assumes that his methods and conclusions have more than a limited role, he tends to become religious about the matter, ascribing total appreciative awareness to the manner in which he has sought to control the otherness of existence. This is quite similar to what happens when people from one race and civilization encounter "others" for the first time. The others must be dealt with; they must be classified, related to our world view, thereby becoming either "savages" or "gods." We then assume that the other's place in the scheme of things is worthy of methods and actions dependent upon our classification of the other and our conviction about the encounter. What we observe, therefore, is that human beings treat the encounter with the mystery of otherness in various ways. Generally speaking, however, they tend to make a religious foreclosure on the mystery, based on either fear or the need to control. True understanding of the nature of the encounter would lead to a religious openness rather than foreclosure.

Scholars of religion should not base their enterprise on the same kind of religious foreclosure that is symbolized by Ahab and often found in the practice of many religions and in the academic world in general. There should be in us no rage against otherness based on the fear of our inability to control. The fear of the other is the fear of authority. Everything that exists, exists in relationship to others. Our identity—physical and spiritual—is derived from such relationships.

Our continued pursuit of meaning, fulfillment, and knowledge takes place in reference to multifarious otherness. But because we rarely acknowledge in openness the mystery of the others we encounter, we tend to be fearful, defensive, and hostile. We retreat into the delusions of *self*-realization and privatization. Every being has a source, an author; therefore authority is inescapable. The scholar of religion should be aware of this, perhaps more than others, and it should affect his teaching and his scholarship.

Robert N. Bellah, in a discussion of "Religious Studies as 'New Religion,' " observes that

> the necessity to teach a specific tradition reflects a basic assumption of religious studies: man is an inveterately traditional animal. *All efforts to undercut and deny tradition have resulted only in a formation of semi-surreptitious new traditions.* Indeed, when each of us defines who he is, he does so by citing or alluding to certain authorities. This involuntary intellectual genuflection happens in spite of our notion of individuality, of being free from authority and pursuing truth without presuppositions. For even in being free from authority, we indicate those authorities who have helped us become free of authority. It is, therefore, as impossible to be wholly untraditional as it is to be wholly unreligious.[2]

The American experience, of course, has spawned such notions of reclusive pragmatism—that we are what in our seclusion we make of ourselves. We have been a nation of levelers, cutting everything down to our own imaginary proportions. Our leveling distortion of democracy has been derived from a host of social and intellectual factors, not the least of which are the frontier, Puritanism, and the American version of the Enlightenment. From the frontier we learned a rather undiscerning self-sufficiency. Puritanism served us notice of the equalizing power of experience over every other form of association, while the Enlightenment taught us the rational supremacy of every person's thoughts and rights, a supremacy that required us to destroy the legitimacy of all other authority. What we have not been so quick to learn is that these assumptions have a source, therefore an authority. We do not set ourselves absolutely free by challenging authority;

---

[2]Jacob N. Needleman and George Baker, eds., *Understanding the New Religions* (New York: The Seabury Press, 1978) 108; italics added.

we simply carry out the agenda of another authority. Everything that is exists in relationship to others. It is this relationship that serves as authority for our existence. We can either be open, creatively and critically aware of the other, or we can fear the other and rage against all authority.

There is authority in religious studies. It is found in the traditions we examine, in the canons and warrants of analysis and criticism to which we subscribe, but also in the very mystery of otherness that confronts us. The other as author must be respected, even loved, by the scholar of religion, for he knows that his enterprise is not in any way superior to the truth of those teachings and symbols that manifest the traditions of otherness. The other must be allowed to speak. He or she is a mystery that cannot be slain by the harpoons of Ahab.

Often the scholar of religion fears the otherness he investigates because it represents a power he does not have. When the American Indians encountered the white man on the Western plains, they discovered power (medicine) that they did not possess. The white man seemed to come in ever-greater numbers. He had great quantities of manufactured goods. The first response was fear, with its attendant dispositions of retreat, observation, ambush, robbery, and assault. But the native soon became wise. He concluded from his own traditional thinking that all power was part of one's world view. All power is religious and is available if one can find a way to make it part of one's understanding of the world. So the Nez Percés initiated a famous journey to St. Louis so

> that they too could learn something of the white man's medicine. . . . "Medicine" is best thought of as "power," and in the Indian's metaphysics power was an attribute of every creature, object, and operation, if only you could find out how to use it; a subsidiary meaning of "mystery" is almost inseparable from "power." The Nez Percés understood that white medicine centered, as Indian medicine did, in religion. When they decided to ask for instruction in religion, they wanted to increase their magical control of nature in order to acquire objects which the white man possessed or knew how to make. . . . They were altogether uninterested in Christian spirituality, morality, or salvation: they were satisfied with what they had.[3]

---

[3]Bernard De Voto, *Across the Wide Missouri* (Boston: Houghton Mifflin Company, 1947) 13.

I do not believe that human nature among modern intellectuals and academics is substantially different from that of the native Americans of the nineteenth century. We, too, discover the evidence of power in the traditions we encounter in the study of religion. We know we do not ourselves possess that power. Our *initial* response, which in the case of many scholars becomes also their *final* response, is one of fear. We have encountered that which we do not have and do not seem able to control. We retreat into some stronghold of rationalistic seclusion from which we observe the manifestations of power. Then we begin assaults on the other, hoping to reduce the strength of its medicine. However, our wisdom is not as practical as that of the Nez Percés. Our understanding is not as great as the fear that we have encountered that which is in some sense superior to our testing. We do not recognize that the power we observe is not available to our assault; it is only accessible by a certain instruction to which we must submit, a certain entrance into the world of the other.

I recall my first encounter with the great writers of Catholic spirituality: Evagrius Ponticus, John Cassian, Gregory of Nyssa, Dionysius the Areopagite, St. Simeon the New Theologian, St. Gregory Palamas, St. Bonaventure, St. Teresa of Avila, St. John of the Cross, the anonymous author of the Cloud of Unknowing—*the list is much longer. I shall take one example, this from St. Teresa of Avila, a sixteenth-century Spanish Carmelite:*

> *Though I saw that He was speaking to me, and though I was looking upon that great beauty of His, and experiencing the sweetness with which He uttered those words—sometimes stern words—with the most lovely and Divine Mouth, and though, too, I was extremely desirous of observing the colour of His eyes, or His height, so that I should be able to describe it, I have never been sufficiently worthy to see this, nor has it been of any use for me to attempt to do so; if I tried, I lost the vision altogether. Though I sometimes see Him looking at me compassionately, His gaze has such power that my soul cannot endure it and remains in so sublime a rapture that it loses this beauteous vision in order to have the greater fruition of it all. It is clear that the Lord wants of us only humility and shame, our acceptance of what is given us and our praise of its Giver.*
> *There is nothing that we can do about [such visions]; we cannot see more or less of them at will; and we neither call them up nor banish*

*them by our efforts. The Lord's will is that we shall see quite clearly that
they are produced, not by us but by His Majesty.*[4]

*I have chosen this rather lengthy passage in order to give ample il-
lustration to the description of an experience, accompanied by a perfectly orderly perspective on the matter. When I first confronted this kind
of literature and the curious power it embodied, I made an automatic
retreat into rationalistic seclusion. Several assumptions were at work
somewhere in the back of my brain. Perhaps such words were "mere
poetry"; perhaps they were the product of some unbalanced mind; perhaps the words were deliberately intended to mislead or mesmerize;
perhaps they were the result of a now-antiquated way of thinking.*

*Whatever the correct assumption, there was no doubt of accounting
for this phenomenon on some other terms. It did not occur to me that the
passage could possibly refer to anything understandable in its own
terms. My own initial retreat into rationalistic seclusion was caused in
part by my fear of a power that I did not have and could not understand.
As an honest scholar, I must recognize that fear of power and be prepared to understand it in ways that transcend the methods and attitudes
I am accustomed to rely upon. I cannot manipulate such knowledge; I
can only learn it. The other must be free to be whatever it is. It must be
encountered on its own terms. I must be open to its potential; and in order to do that, I must come (like the Nez Percés) for instruction.*

The fear of authority and fear of power in our encounter with otherness lead the scholar of religion to assume that the other can be
bracketed. Bracketing is the technique we devise in order to manage
what is unmanageable. To bracket is to suspend the vitality of our encounter with the other so that we may examine a selected segment of
what was said or done in the encounter. The process of bracketing requires that the other be static. The other must be still and know that
we are god. The only thing we can bracket is outward appearance—
in fact, the outward appearance of a moment or two in the encounter.
We must establish a "phenomenon" in order to observe, measure, and
analyze. The very nature of the more acceptable forms of scholarly inquiry requires this of us. Yet human religiousness is expressive of the

---

[4]David A. Fleming, ed., *The Fire and the Cloud* (New York: Paulist Press, 1978) 223-
24.

fact that we are constantly confronted with a reality that stands in *living* relationship to us. There is an *other* who makes claims on us and allows us to make claims of our own. Religious studies must not assume it is understanding religion by bracketing; rather, it is understanding only the static realities it has "manufactured" in order to conduct its inquiry.

Walter Capps, in an essay on "The Interpretation of New Religion and Religious Studies," has put it this way:

> Religious Studies was constructed upon a set of interrelated Enlightenment convictions, which can be readily identified: (1) objects of investigations have essences, which are discrete and unchangeable; (2) religion can be routinely investigated by the scientific method; (3) an agreed-upon sense of "objectivity" makes truth publicly or commonly accessible, regardless of what the subject is; (4) analysis can be separated from attitudes; and (5) dispassionateness is a fit mode of scholarly inquiry, most able to make truth accessible. *All of these assumptions presume the cardinal one, which is that clarity appears through the process of breaking things down into smaller and smaller pieces.*[5]

But such assumptions are challenged by the nature of religion, and we have begun to be aware of the lingering hegemony of Enlightenment methods. Bracketing assumes that a segment of experience, separated for analysis, gives the scholar an effective knowledge of *homo religiosus*. Presumably this means that the "discrete and unchangeable essences," of which Capps speaks, function as microcosm. Religious knowledge itself, however, tends to assume that one must know the macrocosm in order to know the significance and structure of the microcosm. There are signs, of course, that we are in the process of recognizing the weakness of traditional scholarly activity that relies heavily on Enlightenment precepts. In religious studies itself, however, there tends to be a lag at this point. Scholars of religion are too afraid that their colleagues will think them "religious." They are too apprehensive of the unique nature of their enterprise and they want to be certain they are fully accepted and credentialed members of the academic establishment.

---

[5]Walter H. Capps, in Needleman and Baker, *Understanding the New Religions*, 104; italics added.

At times the degree of our tractability achieves almost comic proportions. We are so anxious to receive the approval of historians, sociologists, philosophers, and anthropologists that we neglect the particularity of our discipline. We might very well disperse ourselves into those disciplines from which we seek approbation.

In the preface to Across the Wide Missouri, *Bernard De Voto tells of emancipating himself from the pedantry of his betters. He refers to the practice of having used the spelling of Indian plurals that the guild of ethnologists imposes.*

> *It seems that when you bring Indian tribal names into English from the mother tongue, the plural has the same form as the singular. The ethnologist's medicine has commanded him in a vision to stand on those plurals, even when they are clearly English words, and neither logic nor a decent sensitiveness to style will move him to violate the sacred teaching. Up to now I have followed his precept, forcing myself to write not only "twenty-one Arapaho" but also "thirty-eight Crow" and even, God help us, "one hundred and two Blackfoot." But at last I have encountered an ethnologist who is willing to defy the Rules Committee, and one is all I need. "There is no more sense," George E. Hyde writes, "in writing 'seven Oglala' than in writing 'seven Spaniard' or 'seven Western state.' " Check. I intend to write "Blackfeet" from now on.*[6]

Perhaps the sign that we need in order to have courage to defy the rules committee in religious studies is offered by certain scholars who concern themselves with biblical hermeneutics. Professor Joseph Sittler, a theologian dealing with the subject of "grace" in the Scriptures, suggests the need for a hermeneutic "fully appropriate to the way the community of faith bore witness in the words of Scripture, most rich in that potential for hearing and obedience which has in fact been the force of biblical speech for centuries, and most congruent with *that* 'living Word' *to which the Church gives proper praise."*[7] *This statement reflects a sensitivity to the dynamic reality of our religiousness—a reality that cannot be bracketed. Check. I intend to be scholarly in a way that is "most congruent with that living Word" from now on.*

---

[6]De Voto, *Across the Wide Missouri*, xiii-xiv.

[7]Joseph Sittler, *Essays on Nature and Grace* (Philadelphia: Fortress Press, 1972) 41; italics added.

James E. Huchingson, in an essay in the *Journal of the American Academy of Religion*, explores the possibility of using "general system theory" for the development of a doctrine of God. In doing so, he scores another point on behalf of the need to discover an approach to religious studies that is appropriate to the nature of human religiousness and the religions that communicate it. Huchingson writes of the assumption underlying the established method of analysis—"that the nature and truth of reality are to be found in ultimate simples, the smallest units comprising a phenomenon." He goes on to suggest that systems theorists tend to see things as organized wholes.

> They base their inquiry upon the complex and dynamic interaction of elements which, when taken together rather than taken apart, disclose far more about the ways a thing behaves than isolated particles ever could. Hegel's dictum *Das Wahre ist das Ganza* (the true is the whole) is the sum of the systems position.[8]

A concern for the whole leads to a radical catholicity that is dissatisfied with the assumption that one has understood religion by reducing it to small and static proportions. A concern for the whole will be constantly aware of the fact that the dynamic nature of the reality of otherness makes requirements of us even as we seek to study and understand it. The truth we encounter in otherness is of a whole; it cannot be claimed or fabricated. It must be received and discerned.

No doubt scholars will always rage against otherness. They will always tend to be very much more like Ahab than Ishmael. After all, that seems to be a dominant facet of human nature itself—to fear what is unmanageable; to seek to be autonomous, creating our own universe. Therefore, we shall continue to become methodologists.

Methodology must be distinguished from method. There is no denying the need for methods to approach and to describe any particular moment in our encounter with otherness. This we cannot escape. But concern for method tends to become so fascinating an enterprise for some that it may assume the proportions of ideology. Pragmatic necessity becomes a matter of life and death. Method becomes methodology—a virtual belief system in the obsessive rage against the

---

[8]James E. Huchingson, "The World as God's Body: A Systems View," *Journal of the American Academy of Religion* 48:3 (September 1980): 336-37.

otherness we struggle to control. So long as the other can be kept in a museum or strapped to a work table, we are not faced with the dynamism of its being. Thus we shall continue to excite ourselves by the discovery of some principle or image-system derived from the work of anthropologists and sociologists. The excitement will be beneficial if we remember the limitations of the discovery, if we refuse to "believe" in it. Otherwise, it becomes one more chapter in our attempt to slay the great white mystery.

Religious studies must develop an approach that is open to the knowledge that, by its nature, otherness offers certain things to us. For this to happen, we must be able to rise above the methods we feel compelled to employ in our study of religiousness and its many incarnations. I should like to suggest that we keep before our minds a certain grammar for the study of religion. A grammar includes the schemes and the rules for the use of a language. Sometimes people use a language well without being very familiar with its grammar. Presumably, one who knows a grammar well does not think about it very much unless he is a grammarian. But religious studies is so new that its grammar is still being formed. The language is the language of the *study* of *religion*. What we must do is describe the important principles, regardless of the *methods* we use or the areas we survey.

Succeeding chapters of this book will seek to explore more fully the understanding of religion as the elaborated expression of our encounter with otherness; then to examine the shape of religious studies as the contemplation of otherness, as a mode of critical inquiry that will enable us to be open to the uniqueness of the dynamic reality being studied. This amounts to saying that religious studies itself calls for a hermeneutic derived from a contemplation of otherness—one that balances its analytical necessities by way of deference to certain attitudes and rules imputable to the nature of religion. What has been attempted in this chapter is to describe the dilemma of religious studies, to point to those attitudes among many scholars of religion that tend to deform the subject we study. It is necessary to risk repetition in order to say that religious studies is an unformed discipline partly because it is a new discipline and partly because it may be characteristic of the dynamic reality of the encounter with otherness. There has been an anxiety among us, an urge to make the enterprise secure.

It is hoped that some of the reasons for that anxiety have been described.

A religious text is always concerned with *transformed* existence. Openness to the other effects transformation. The text has to do, therefore, with a form of seeing and hearing—of thinking—that is different from the ordinary. The text is already the *product* of that transformation. It is somewhat beside the mark to examine that text with the assumptions of the ordinary mind. At least it is quite useless to *leave* the task of understanding with the results of those assumptions. I may not need to be a so-called "believer" to read the text, but I am required to find a way to understand what is read, to make it the content of my thought world, to remember that it speaks to me from beyond my ordinary understanding. A Sufi tale can be a humorous story, which I submit to various forms of literary and historical analysis; but unless I wander (with wonder) into its transforming levels, I have not studied it as a scholar of religion. I must be like Ishmael, not like Ahab. What Ahab misses in his relentless search for conquest is what religion has traditionally known as contemplation.

Contemplation enhances and intensifies ordinary rational thought and analysis. Austin Farrer suggests that poetry may sometimes breed too much fancy and egotism; love may sometimes breed animality and complacency. Yet both lover and poet at least *look at something and see it.* "And," says Farrer, "the chief impediment to religion in this age, I often think, is that no one ever looks at anything at all: not so as to *contemplate it*, to apprehend what it is to be that thing, and plumb, if he can, the deep fact of its individual existence."[9]

The task of contemplating the other as a legitimate direction of religious studies is the errand to which this book commits itself.

---

[9]Austin Farrer, *Reflective Faith* (Grand Rapids: Eerdmans, 1972) 37-38.

II / The Contours
of Otherness:
The Singular Other

When I was young, in a time of boyhood marked by a world as fresh and green and utterly marvelous as the day of its creation, I found myself attracted by a huge tropical shell which lay upon my aunt's dressing table. The twentieth century was scarcely a decade old, and people did not travel or collect as they do now. My uncle and aunt lived far inland in the central states and what wandering relative had given them the beautiful iridescent shell I do not know. It was held up to my youthful ear and I was told to listen carefully and I would hear the sea. Out of the great shell, even in that silent bedroom, I, who had never seen the ocean, heard the whispered sibilance, the sigh of waves upon the beach, the little murmurs of moving water, the confused mewing of gulls in the sun-bright air. It was my first miracle, indeed perhaps my first awareness of the otherness of nature, of myself outside, in a sense, and listening, as though beyond light-years, to a remote event. Perhaps, in that Victorian bedroom, with its knickknacks and curios, I had suddenly fallen out of the nature I inhabited and turned, for the first time to survey her with surprise. [1]

Behind all religions lurks the concept of nature. It persists equally in the burial cults of Neanderthal man, in Cro-Magnon hunting art, in the questions of Job and in the answering voice from the whirlwind. In the

---

[1] Loren Eiseley, *The Star Thrower* (New York: Harcourt Brace Jovanovich, Inc., 1978) 216-17.

*end it is the name of man's attempt to define and delimit his world,
whether seen or unseen. He knows intuitively that nature is a reality
which existed before him and will survive his individual death. He may
include in his definition that which is, or that which may be. Nature remains an otherness which incorporates man, but which man instinc-
tively feels contains secrets denied to him.*[2]

Loren Eiseley was an anthropologist, a scientist, and a
profound humanist. His literary style added a powerful intuitive di-
mension to the communication of his ideas. I have been impressed
with the manner in which his writings contain allusions to existence
as the encounter with otherness. There is, of course, no systematic exploration of that otherness. What we learn from Eiseley is that the discovery of otherness is fresh and surprising at each instant. We learn
that the very personal and private experience of otherness is the beginning of *self*-awareness, but that such self-awareness is part of a
greater whole. We sense being outside, looking in and listening; at the
same time, there is the perception of being inside, looking out. We are
aware that we transcend that which we seem to be. The discovery of
otherness is the discovery of the More-Than-in-the-Midst.

There is no such thing as nature. It is a name that results from the
discovery that one stands outside, looking in on the whole of which we
are apparently a part. Scientifically we seek to probe the secrets of this
otherness that incorporates us. How does this "nature" work? In what
ways may we control and utilize the secret? Religiously we seek to respond, to relate the self to the greatest possible range of otherness
that is revealed to us. What is the meaning of the self in relation to the
other? Are there ways in which the self may improve its understanding
of otherness, and be transformed by a more integral relationship?
Both science and religion are acknowledgments of existence as the encounter with otherness.

Much of the encounter has to do with the singular and personal di-
mension of existence. To examine the contours of otherness is to investigate the awareness of the self in its relationship with what seem
to be individuals. A great deal of our existence is spent contending
with what it means to discover who we are and what we must do in

---

[2]Ibid., 225.

relation to the other person, the other thing. Who am I in relation to this other whom I meet? Paul Tillich writes:

> Man's self-affirmation has two sides which are distinguishable but not separable; one is in the affirmation of the self as a self; that is of a separated, self-centered, individualized, incomparable, free self-determining self. This is what one affirms in every act of self-affirmation.[3]

But such self-affirmation is always done by reference to an other, or others, of whom one is a part and *from* whom one must be distinguished. That is why Tillich also found it necessary to say:

> But the self is self only because it has a world, a structured universe, to which it belongs and from which it is separated at the same time. Self and world are correlated, and so are individualization and participation. For this is just what participation means: being a part of something from which one is, at the same time, separated.[4]

It is this personal, self-discovering, encounter with otherness that accounts for the quest, the journey, the pilgrimage, the search for salvation, and the heightened experience of alternative reality that tend to be part of the structure of all religious traditions and experience. Certainly we seek because we become aware of the fact that we see from outside and inside ourselves simultaneously. To become aware of an other outside oneself is to discover that selfhood is somehow dependent upon relationship to others. And so one begins the quest for meaningful communication with others by way of insight, sensation, and thought. William James has commented that

> in the dog's life we see the world invisible to him because we live in both worlds. In human life, although we only see our world, and his within it, yet encompassing both these worlds a still wider world may be there, as unseen by us as our world is by him.[5]

The need to act as if that world were there and to ritualize its presence accounts for human religiousness in the pursuit of everything we do, whether it be science, liturgy, or storytelling. That world is present be-

---

[3]Paul Tillich, *The Courage to Be* (New Haven: Yale University Press, 1952, 1972) 86.

[4]Ibid., 87-88.

[5]William James, "Is Life Worth Living?" *New World Metaphysics*, ed. Giles Gunn (New York: Oxford University Press, 1981) 308.

cause even in the act of seeing our world, as James put it, we are seeing something other-than-ourselves that somehow *includes* us.

The scholarly study of religion is not all that different from being involved in the pursuit of and expression of one's own religiousness. Both sets of thought and action result from the variety of encounters with otherness, which makes us explorers and pilgrims. We want to understand, to celebrate, and to investigate the implications of our commitments. Much recent scholarship in religious studies has relied at some point on the expressions of religion termed by Joachim Wach *verbal*, *practical*, and *social*.[6] The verbal expression refers to the mythic or doctrinal forms in which the tradition is clarified or passed on. The practical refers to the practices of ritual, liturgy, and code that exist in tandem with the verbal. The social expression is the form of community, the structures of leadership and teaching, that is fundamental to the tradition. Robert Ellwood has suggested that the absence of any one of these three expressions indicates that the phenomena we may be observing do not constitute a religious tradition.[7] I have some reservations about the appropriateness of the Wachian terminology, but have no qualms concerning the need for a classification of the expressions of religion, along with a concern for their integral relationships.

Are not these expressions of human religiousness somewhat parallel to the study of religion itself? We begin the study of religion with a set of assumptions and convictions. Even if we delay the inevitable pursuit of a definition of religion, we conduct our business with an intuitive sense of what it is we are studying. Furthermore, in some cases we work with at least a functional or hypothetical set of organized principles that will help us construct a method of study. A kind of intuitive response to the otherness that incorporates us immediately seeks other forms of reason (faith in search of understanding). Sometimes this enterprise waxes into methodology, which is really the acceptance of some ideology as essential to the task. In other words, a certain system of ideas about what is true forms a doctrinal base for

---

[6]Joachim Wach, *The Comparative Study of Religions* (New York: Columbia University Press, 1958) passim.

[7]Robert S. Ellwood, Jr., *Religious and Spiritual Groups in Modern America* (Englewood Cliffs: Prentice-Hall, Inc., 1973) 31.

our activity. In addition to principles and methodologies, we usually also have a vision, a set of images, that motivates us as scholars and serves as a guide for our work. These images may be from among those inevitably shared by the culture in which we reside, or they may be derived from the literature we accept as seminal. For example, the recent turn to anthropology for methods that may be useful to the study of religion has produced a rich imaginal lore that almost amounts to a mythology. We are now encountering words such as "liminal."[8] Every word becomes flesh of some sort; it produces an image, particularly if it is recited frequently in the corridors of academe and the chambers of professional societies.

Liminality began as a concept devised by anthropologists to indicate marginality. In the transitions of our existence, there is a middle or "threshold" phase that is "between the times" of the past and future states.[9] During this liminal phase human behavior and characteristics are different from those of the parenthetical phases. Doubtless, this is very helpful to some scholars, although any effective historian or biographer could certainly discover the same truth without showing mounting reverence before the new icon that has asserted its presence. After a while, liminality becomes a "thing," an object. At that point the question must always be: has it ceased to be useful; has it begun to get in the way of the continuing struggle to see things as they are (which, I take it, is the purpose of all learning)?

The point is that images are inevitably formed, all along the pathway of scholarship and learning. Liminality becomes a thing in itself because human beings "see things" even when they propose the most abstract concept or set forth a heuristic device. The further point is that the study of religion devises mythology and symbolism as well as doctrinal schemes. The result begins to look suspiciously like the verbal expression of human religiousness. While this is unavoidable, the awareness of what is happening is extremely important. Ishmael sits loose to the truth of it; Ahab becomes obsessed with sharpening it into a harpoon wherewith to slay the mysterious other.

---

[8]Cf. Victor Turner, *The Ritual Process* (Ithaca: Cornell University Press, 1977).

[9]Ibid., 95.

What has been said of the verbal expression is similarly true of the practical. Does not the scholar of religion find himself engaged in certain ritual actions that are not entirely explained in terms of the mechanical necessities of his profession? His conversations with colleagues may be an attempt to learn, to gain the benefit of another's experience, or to seek cooperation in a common venture. However, it readily takes on ritual modes. The language begins to be as much concerned with the recitation of an appropriate *dhikr*[10] as with the pursuit of truth and its methods. Words such as "liminality" become part of the rhythm of remembrance, whereby scholars seek to touch base with what is real to them. There are many other such words, of course; part of their use stems from academics' love-hate relationship to certain saints: today one cannot fail to hear the eloquent ritual deference to Turner, Ricoeur, Gadamer, and others. The colloquia in which faculty share ideas and the results of study are as much a ritual enactment as they are an actual sharing of information. Time and space forbid much comment about professional meetings as ritual events—great festivals in which certain things occur according to established order, with just the right amount of creative contribution to provide promise as well as security. By extension, much of present-day academic publishing is totally meaningless *unless* it is considered as essentially ritualistic.

When we turn to social expression, the observations are easy to make. There exists a variety of initiatory stages through which the scholar must move, both in preparation for entry into the circle of adepts and in establishing himself with acceptance once inside. The social order of the study of religion is rigorously controlled by such processes as "refereeing," as it relates to publication, placement, promotion, "grantsmanship," and lecturing. A curious orthodoxy asserts itself from local conventicles to national councils. This is not said to prove that the study of religion is itself a religion. It may very well be that the Wachian forms of religious expression require further elaboration. Perhaps they should be challenged. The point is that the scholar does not escape the experience of otherness even in his most pretentious efforts to study its implications.

---

[10]Dhikr is an Islamic and Sufi term denoting a word or exercise used to "remember" Allah, or to call forth the reality of God.

Why do people study religion? An acceptable reply is that they study it because it exists and needs to be understood like everything else in this world. But there are more covert reasons as well. Virtually everyone who begins the study does so out of curiosity as to whether the great traditions, with their sages and priests and spiritual masters, had knowledge and experience not ordinarily available. One wants to know, what is this business of religion all about, and is there anything in it for me? Could it be that there is a special way of relating to the mystery of otherness that incorporates me? Shall I dismiss it as superstition or *poesis*, or has it something to do with the highest creative level of my humanity? Elaboration of the mystery has led to many forms and expressions throughout history. Scholars seek to use historical, social-scientific, and philosophical skills to examine these elaborations called religions. But if there is a trace of Ishmael in their veins, they will suspect that what they are dealing with is more than their methods reveal; indeed, they will begin to be amazed by the mystery, and wonder whether their response to otherness needs nurturing.

Early on, infants become aware of themselves as they begin to observe the presence of an other whose loving attention contributes to their well-being. A great deal hinges on that encounter. The nature of the other's care—its peculiarities, uniqueness, its kindness, or its indifference—will blend with the infant's response to effect the patterns of selfhood and salvation that will be a continuing characteristic of the mature person. The encounters of otherness are always dialectical: the personal does not exist without the other, and the other exists only in relationship to the personal. It is not a matter of the self *or* the other; it is always the self *and* the other in relationship. As Martin Buber explained it: "there is not I as such but only the I of the basic word I-You and the I of the basic word I-It. When a man says I, he means one or the other. The I he means is present when he says I. And when he says You or It, the I of one or the other basic word is also present."[11] The initial and persistent level of the encounter with otherness tends to be the singular personal. That is, we are very early aware of singular others and throughout our lives we continue to respond in varied ways to them. Sometimes we see the other as a benefactor, as a bearer of good

---

[11]Martin Buber, *I and Thou* (New York: Charles Scribner's Sons, 1970) 54.

will. The other is one whose presence does well by us. Presumably, in a good familial setting, the benefactor is initially known in the encounter with the mother and father. Good has come to us, we are secure and hopeful as a result of the fact that others exist *for us* in certain respects. These unique others are outside of us, yet within us in ways that make for our well-being.

Of course, there are numerous other faces of the singular other as benefactor. It may be someone who gives of himself as a teacher, a friend, an employer, a priest, or a physician. Or we may encounter the benefactor in that other who becomes lover, with whom we experience a union that is pleasurable and meaning-giving, supportive of our very existence. Relationships to others who meet us as benefactors will determine in some measure our own spontaneous ability to be benefactor with others. If we remember that the other always becomes a part of our own selfhood, then it is clear that the greater the encounter with others as benefactor, the more likely our own selfhood will assume a similar face.

There are also encounters with the singular other as malefactor. If an other as person or as object (thing) is the source of suffering or grievance, we have a need to understand who or what this other is for reference in future relationships. We certainly know that this other is potentially a cause of harm or evil. We may conclude that the encounter is of such intensity and significance that we shall always think of this other as malefactor. Of course, no one is absolute malefactor, just as no one is absolute benefactor. Even when we deal with symbols of reality such as Satan or God, we are not dealing with absolutes. If we think of them as such, it is because our minds will not accept the fact that no other is entirely "out there" somewhere as an exteriorized object. Every other is related to us, and in us as well as outside of us.

Meanwhile, the discovery of the other as malefactor may be the occasion for us to think of him/her/it as enemy, as threat to our well-being. To us, this other will tend to wear the mask of evil. The reason for this response may result from an insufficient encounter with others as benefactors. As a result, any meeting with an other that thwarts our wholeness will be considered an occasion of evil or threat. Of course, it is also true that many individuals (whether persons or things) are inevitably cast in the role of malefactor because they are most frequently encountered in that way. Someone whose life from adolescence through adulthood is devoted to crime and violence is likely to be stereotyped as a malefactor simply because society and the individual are aware of the predominance of malefaction in his behavior. The rattlesnake and the Cholla cactus may be invested with certain aesthetic qualities at times, but we are likely to think of them as malefactors because they are frequently encountered as harmful.

In Isaac Singer's novel Satan in Goray *there is a young woman who is the cause of much speculation and hysteria as the people of a small Polish shtetl prepare for the coming of the Messiah, sometime during the year 1666. Rechele is seventeen years old, has a lame foot, and is seldom seen in public. "She was tall, with a greenish complexion, but handsome, with long black hair that hung down to her waist." People had tried to arrange a match for her, but her father had never responded.*

> *Besides, Rechele's behavior was strange from the beginning. When it thundered she would scream and hide under the bed. To the young wives and girls who came to call on her she said nothing, driving them away with her indifference. From early morning to night she sat alone, knitting stockings or reading in the Hebrew volumes she had brought from abroad. Sometimes she would stand at the window braiding her hair. Her large, dark eyes gazed beyond the rooftops—wide-open, brilliant, as though seeing things concealed from others. Though Rechele had a deformity, she aroused sinful thoughts in men.*

Then one day Rechele was visited by the Angel Sandalfon and she began to prophesy in a voice that could be heard throughout the town of Goray. Afterward she collapsed and was carried to the dais in the study hall, as though she were the sacred Torah. "Some even touched her with their fingertips as she passed and bore their fingers to their lips, as when a scroll is taken from the Ark."[12]

Rechele was a mysterious person. She had remained largely unknown and silent until the time when she began to serve as the vessel, the voice for the announcement of Messiah's coming. There is an element of the unknown in every encounter with an other, but some encounters tend to be dominated by mystery. This gives rise to encounter with the singular other as mystery. The less of these encounters we have, the greater the potential for investing the experi-

---

[12]Isaac Bashevis Singer, *Satan in Goray* (New York: Fawcett Crest, 1980) 17-18.

ence with agnostic and eccentric significance. If the unknown is simply accepted as basic to *every* encounter with otherness, there is likely to be creative response. If it is embraced as some exterior objective reality that is foreign to us, then the response is likely to be exotic or credulous. The first response is worshipful and reverential, the second magical. The point is that the encounter with the singular other is always an occasion of mystery, but we tend to recognize it only in the more objective forms that appeal to or perhaps repulse our imaginations.

Every awareness of an other is accompanied by a characterization and a naming. The other comes into clear existence only as we name it and begin to characterize it. Rechele, as a focus of the mysterious other, takes seriously her own peculiarities and permits herself to become the instrument of the people's expectations and her own frustration. She becomes the exotic prophetess, the harbinger of the end of suffering and the beginning of a new era. In a somewhat similar fashion, Ahab fixes upon the curious elusory element in the great whale.

> This elusive quality it is, which causes the thought of whiteness, when divorced from more kindly associations, and coupled with any object terrible in itself, to heighten that terror to the furthest bounds. Witness the white bear of the poles, and the white shark of the tropics; what but their smooth, flaky whiteness makes them the transcendent beings they are? . . . Bethink thee of the albatross, whence come those clouds of spiritual wonderment and pale dread, in which that white phantom sails in all imaginations? Not Coleridge first threw that spell, but God's great unflattering laureate, Nature.[13]

Ishmael speculates about whiteness and concludes that the albino whale is the symbol of all human apprehensions in the face of nothingness and otherness.[14] To Ahab the mystery of the white whale is a combination of awe and fear and anger—a symbol of madness. The enigma of his own selfhood in a world of others with whom he must contend finds its focus in the mysterious whiteness of the whale. The whale is a creature of great range and power, of mildness and ferocity.

---

[13]Herman Melville, *Moby Dick* (New York: The Modern Library, 1950) 188-89.

[14]Ibid., 195.

In a similar fashion, each of us encounters others whose peculiarities match the uncertainties in our own sense of self.

The first European to set foot on the shores of America was a person who did not know what to expect. Would this be a hostile or an encouraging environment? Would it be the restored Garden or the ominous Wilderness? The abode of Adam or the habitation of the Evil One? His own bewilderment and vulnerability, curiously fed by the world he had left, found focus in the natives whom he met. These people were very unusual in color, costume, and custom. The encounter with these others was an occasion of great mystery. Columbus wrote that

> the inhabitants of both sexes . . . go always naked as they were born, as soon however as they see that they are safe, and have laid aside all fear, they are very simple and honest, and exceedingly liberal with all they have. . . . They exhibit great love towards all others in preference to themselves.[15]

On the other hand, Columbus had already taken some of these people by force in order to teach them his language. These mysterious creatures had to be characterized and named. For some Europeans, the encounter was more benign than fearful; the other became a simple creature of nature—to be looked after and in some sense emulated. However, there were also those for whom the creature of the wilderness was a threat, perhaps an enemy. In either case, his tawny color, his nakedness, and his customs had a great deal to do with naming him Indian and characterizing him as a rather naive child of nature: the creature of the restored Garden, rather than the sinister denizen of the Wilderness.

There were other encounters among Europeans and native Americans that had different results. Expectations, preconceptions, and adverse circumstances created a contrasting response to the mystery. Therefore, differences in appearance and customs gave rise to characterizations and namings of another kind. The native became savage, cannibal, worshiper of Satan; the European became alien, white devil, despoiler, and sometimes, of course, a white god because of the power

---

[15]Christopher Columbus, "Letter of Lord Raphael Sanchez, Treasurer to Ferdinand and Isabella, King and Queen, on His First Voyage," *New World Metaphysics*, ed. Gunn, 7.

associated with his arrival, his inventions, and his strange-seeming albinism.

This suggests another element in the profile of the singular other. The other is known as benefactor, malefactor, and mystery; but he or she is frequently encountered as power. While power of some kind is implicit in all characterizations of the other, there are the distinctive occasions when we are most vividly aware of its presence. Whether it be for good or ill, we are confronted with potency. Certainly mysterious, it is not just mystery, for it demands an almost immediate adjustment from us. We must respond in a decisive manner. We may be filled with a curious blending of fear, wonder, attraction, and foreboding. Still, something is *expected* of us, some action. There is no experience of power that is not due to the encounter with otherness. To be aware of power is to be aware of an other whom we may avoid or try to befriend in order to utilize power for our own ends.

When red man met white man, much of the mystery of the encounter had to do with the discovery of power, which required some response. Frequently the native American observed the white man's power of weaponry and mobility, his superior equipment, and came to the conclusion that this power could be available to him if only he could learn the ritual truths of the white man. But in the case of the Bean people of southern Arizona, the Papagos, there was the rich heritage of desert life in which every encounter was with the raw powers of existence. Corn, roots, seeds, cacti, deer, rabbits, squirrels, and birds—their presence signaled power. "So the Papagos wandered, calm and smiling, back and forth across the waste of brilliant barrenness which Elder Brother, their god, had given them."[16] The Papagos also sang, not simply for self-expression, but as a response to all the powerful others who were part of their existence. They sang in order to induce a proper relationship to such powers.

> In such a community, singing became not only the practical basis of Papago life, but also the most precious possession of the people. The power of song was an honor to be earned; it could not be assumed lightly at the mere whim of an individual. The describing of a desired event in the magic of beautiful speech was to them the means by

[16]Ruth Murray Underhill, *Singing for Power* (Berkeley: University of California Press, 1938, 1976) 3.

which to make that event take place. All their songs described such events. . . . Magic will be worked if the description is vivid and if the singing or recitation is done, as it should be, at the right time and with the right behavior, on behalf of all the people.[17]

The songs were all "songs of power," dramatic presentations of the interaction of the powerful otherness of desert life.

If I am correct in my description of the singular and personal level of the encounter with otherness, then it must be clear that even the activities of a scholar of religion are replete with such meetings. We never wrestle merely with texts, but with that which may do harm or good, confront us with mystery and power. We may pretend to deal with the text as text; in this manner it reveals its otherness as that which we must triumph over, or that which we respond to with warmth, respect, and expectation. Whether it be text, ritual, or social structure, the same observation applies. Hence it is also true that we never encounter any religious phenomenon as a mere object. Of course, we may *pretend* to do so; in such a case, we develop the obsessions of Ahab in his rage against otherness.

The scholar's work is always to a great extent existentially based. He deals with what he wishes to classify as phenomena, but try as he might, the encounter cannot be limited to the effects of bracketing. The scholar's encounter with the other is laden with the experiences of all previous encounters, with his own doubts and expectations. In other words, his own search for integral meaning in relation to all sorts of others is always at stake. What is more, the subtle ways in which texts, rituals, and social structure also communicate their own experience of encounter is always present in our work. That is to say, something of both original and continuing significance is always communicated in a religious phenomenon. Any attempt at a style of critical evaluation that seeks merely to judge the thing itself as a mere artifact of aesthetic or historical consequence will not be very successful.

A dance evolves in the ceremonial life of a people because the sense of otherness in which they are involved could only elicit that particular expression. In order to understand the dance, one must know something of the world view in which benefactors, malefactors,

---

[17]Ibid., 6.

mystery, and power have all found a special place. Additionally, this form of knowing must always ask, What does it mean to know as these people know? To encounter the dance as anything less than this is not to encounter the religious phenomenon at all, merely some superficial structure of action.

In the same manner, the Qur'an is Qur'an. We may perform historical and literary surgery upon its language and its *suras*, but unless we find a way to encounter it as a sacred text, we shall not know it as Qur'an. A religious phenomenon is always a medium of revelation. It has the power of communion with the expressions of otherness that gave it birth. This truth does not mean that one is required to be a "believer" or a member of the tradition that reverences the phenomenon. We must simply learn to *think* (not think *about*) what we read, and to make the phenomenon the content of our experience.

To fail to approach the religious phenomenon with sensitivity to its revelatory power is to pretend that one is not human. It is to rage like Ahab against one's finitude. "Finitude is that limitation of human existence which is not in man but is a sort of boundary between man and man, the self and the world—the experience of otherness thanks to which man stands revealed to himself."[18] Finitude is not so much a limitation as it is a condition. It represents the circumstances of our consciousness, our awareness. Every moment of knowledge of self is at once a knowledge of an other. Self-and-world, man-and-man, are the conditions of existence. It is not, as the existentialists say, that "the limitation of man's powers . . . belongs to the very essence of his existence and that he must live without that comprehensive knowledge that was sought in metaphysics."[19]

Comprehensive knowledge is the understanding that the most real fact of existence is the appositional power of others to reveal us to ourselves. It is somewhat as Josiah Royce put it: "Man can attend to but a very narrow range of facts at any one instant." The span of our consciousness is conditioned by our dialectical relationship to others. Only when repetition makes our encounter with an other become familiar are we in a position to identify something seen or heard. Ac-

---

[18]Gabriel Vahanian, *Wait Without Idols* (New York: George Braziller, Inc., 1964) 55.

[19]John Macquarrie, *Principles of Christian Theology* (New York: Charles Scribner's Sons, 1966, 1977) 23.

cording to Royce, we can attend only to a very few distant others at any one time. This condition is not a defect of any one sense. *But*, says Royce, what is equally true of us is that this conditioned consciousness remembers that it is *otherness* that conditions it. Otherness is open-ended and in relation to the *un*conditioned. "We are always rebelling at our own form of consciousness, so long as we are trying to know or to do anything significant. We want to grasp many things at once, not merely a few." Therefore, says Royce, we constantly view as if our range of consciousness were wider, "as if it were our actual experience, a sense and connection of things."[20] This pragmatic way of ours "depends upon the principle that such a wider view of things, such a larger unity of consciousness, such a direct grasp of the meaning at which we indirectly but ceaselessly aim, *is a reality in the universe*."[21] And, of course, it *is* a reality. There is no way for human existence except to be alive to the comprehensive reality of an open-ended otherness.

We have been exploring one perception, one facet of the contours of otherness. The otherness we observe, but which incorporates us, emerges in our individual and social consciousness in a very singular form. We are aware of encounters with a great multiplicity of others that are the substance of what we sense and what we know. They also have much to do with our own identity. Contending with these others as singular beings, but always finding it necessary to know who and what they are, what they mean, how they relate to us in Royce's "sense and connection of things," we immediately perceive them as benefactors, malefactors, mystery, and power.

---

[20]Josiah Royce, "The Sources of Religious Insight," *New World Metaphysics*, ed. Gunn, 312

[21]Ibid., 315.

III / The Contours of Otherness: The Representative Other

Presupposed by all my sense experience and the judgements arising from it is what I call the certainty of existence—the certainty that I exist as the subject of my experience and that I exist together with other, fellow creatures like myself, with whom I am related and on whose actions I am dependent, even as they are thus related and dependent with respect to me.[1]

Do you know why the stupid Swabians before they decide a matter say, "We must count noses?" This is the story.

Thirteen Swabians were travelling through the country in a group. One day they got the notion that one of their number was missing. To find out whether all were there they took to counting. The first one counted: "This is me; so you are one; you are two"; and so on until the last who was twelve.
"Huh! There are only twelve of us!" said the one who had counted.
"You're wrong," said another, "let me count."
So he counted: "I am I; you are one; you are two"; and so on until the last who was twelve.
A third Swabian counted, with the same results.

---

[1]Schubert M. Ogden, "How Does God Function in Human Life?" *Christianity and Crisis* 27:8 (15 May 1967): 106.

*They just couldn't agree whether one was missing or not; but to settle
the matter they decided to stick their noses in the mud, and then count
the marks. This they did, and found that all thirteen were present.
"I sort of* thought *we were all here," said one of the Swabians.* [2]

It is very difficult to experience the singular other without
an immediate act of association through which we perceive the other
as representative other. This is because it is true that we exist *together
with others*, as Schubert Ogden points out in his essay, "How Does God
Function in Human Life?" It is likewise true that when we observe certain characteristics that others share, we find it easy to justify gener-
alizations about the other-as-representative. The Germans in
Pennsylvania were spoken of as the "dumb-Dutch" by Benjamin
Franklin. And these Pennsylvania Germans carried to Penn's Woods
the tales of "di dumme Schwowe"—the stupid Swabians, those others
whose marginal existence in the pluralistic milieu of the German
states permitted their peculiar characterization to stand as representative others.

Human consciousness finds it exceedingly difficult to deal with its
encounters with otherness. There is the tendency to blur the distinctive existence of the other, to fuse all individuals into some grand totality. This is the way of much orientalism and mysticism, and of
various philosophical monisms. The existence of the other is felt to be
either illusory or pathological. Otherness is not real, or else it is to be
overcome. However, in addition to such intellectual and mystical blur-
ring, there is the opposite tendency of exclusive definition, which
claims to achieve an absolute and mutual separation of others. This
is, of course, capricious and mistaken. There is no existence without
continuous *encounter* with the other. I exist as a singular other, but the
fact that I am other means that my singularity is qualified by its relationships. As Buber explained it, the "I" is always in hyphenation. Narcissism and certain types of objectivism tend to ignore this fact or are
deliriously incapable of accepting it.

In the world of religion itself, the failure to accept hyphenation and
the constant reality of otherness-in-encounter leads to evangelical

---

[2]Thomas R. Brendle and William S. Troxell, *Pennsylvania German Folk Tales, Leg-
ends, Once-Upon-A-Time Stories, Maxims, and Sayings* (Norristown: Pennsylvania German Society, 1944) 110.

preoccupation with one's own salvation. This is what Nicolas Berdyaev condemned as a "satanic caricature" in the case of Christianity.
He understood this tendency as a transcendental egoism that

> invites human beings to settle down comfortably while other people
> and the world are uncomfortable; it denies responsibility of all for all,
> and rejects the oneness of the created world, the oneness of the cos-
> mos. In the realm of the spirit, there is no self-contained and isolated
> personality. The ethics of personal salvation leads to the destruction
> and overthrow of the ideas of paradise and of the Kingdom of God. Real
> heavenly bliss is impossible for me if I isolate myself from the cosmic
> whole and care about myself only. . . . Hence, individual salvation, or
> salvation of the elect is impossible.[3]

If we were to reflect upon this insight in relation to America, we could
see how the history of American religion has been a constant struggle
between transcendental egoism and the vision of the Kingdom of God.
The Kingdom, as H. Richard Niebuhr taught us, asserts itself as more
than a private or singular vision.[4] It constantly reminds us that our
destiny is bound up with others. While the pietist and evangelical impulses in our history always threaten us with transcendental egoism,
the promises of the Kingdom always disturbed such private wishes
with prophetic claims that included others, especially the poor and
the sick.

It should be established by now that the representative other is as
important as the singular other, that neither really exists without the
other. The trick of existence is learning to deal with the other-as-representative without *reducing* the other to its representative character.
Similarly, it is necessary to accept the singular nature of otherness
without forcing its representative character into exile. Paul Tillich
spoke of these matters as the necessary balance between the courage
to be as oneself and the courage to be as a part. He speaks in psychological terms: "The self is self only because it has a world, a structured
universe, to which it belongs and from which it is separated at the
same time. Self and world are correlated, and so are individualization

---

[3]Matthew Spinka, *Nicolas Berdyaev: Captive of Freedom* (Philadelphia: The Westminster Press, 1950) 149.

[4]H. Richard Niebuhr, *The Kingdom of God in America* (New York: Harper and Brothers, 1937, 1959) passim.

and participation. For this is just what participation means: being a part of something from which one is, at the same time, separated." Of course, the understanding of human existence as encounters with otherness means that the representative character of that otherness (the fact that the other is a part of) requires more than a psychological perspective.

Otherness is cosmological and social, which is why a story is therapeutic. It is not psychological adjustment by way of analysis of a private, experiential realm. The story provides us with the potential for contextual placement of the self in the dramas of otherness. No therapy is ultimately helpful if it contends that the self is an atom of selfhood. Since all existence is hyphenated, the self is always a singular other whose relationship to others is representative. That is, the other with whom we stand in meaningful personal relation is also a self among others. Because we cannot entirely separate this other from that context, she or he becomes for us a representative of some group or class as well as a singular other. The only meaningful expression of this contextual mode of existence is story. The highest form of human creativity is storytelling. When one knows a story that does justice to the widest, most comprehensive sense of the dramas of otherness, a whole and meaningful existence is lived. That is the role of religion— to provide that story. The comprehensive human therapy is religious, not psychological. And the form of communication most congenial to religion is story.

The representative other is an unavoidable aspect of the human encounter with otherness. Each singular other cannot be dealt with as an individually distinct possibility. That is impossible because that singular other exists in various modes of relationships that may be organized into recognizable clusters or sets. Accordingly, I will know you in some measure as that singular other whose personal attractiveness appeals to me, but I will simultaneously know you as woman, professor, Californian, and Jewess. The existence of the representative other is both necessary and unavoidable. Therein lies our grandeur and our misery. There are obviously conditions under which the other appears to be related to us solely as representative. If the meeting is pleasant, then the other may be thought of as pleasant. If the encounter is unpleasant, then the other may be identified in that way. In either case, our experience with that other, whom we hardly know, settles upon his representative character and we shall very likely be inclined to associate the experience with those who share this particular form of representation. It is obviously important to human existence to develop a means of recognizing the dialectic of singular and representative otherness. What is required of us is the wisdom to see that the other is not only singular other, but also representative other.

There is a certain uneasiness that accompanies our discovery that we are not really the self-enclosed and contained unit that mechanical notions of the body permit us to assume. To discover that our selfhood takes place in the context of the dramas of selfhood that go on around us is to learn something that challenges us: I am I only in the encounters of otherness. That discovery, like all revelation, may be an unnerving experience. We may seek refuge in the fact that we belong to this or that representative order, and so find identity and solace. In short, we may acquire premature pride or courage. We may shirk responsibility, goldbrick, feign superiority or helplessness—all because we have sought to escape the singularity of our otherness by seeking sanctuary in representative otherness. We may say, for example, "I am white. White is beautiful. And that's all there is." In seeking such refuge, we neglect the responsibility of learning what our unique and singular center of otherness requires of us. In similar fashion, we may wish to avoid responsibility for the representative nature of otherness by making some curious pretext for insular existence. We may assume that we are ego-contained, that our responsible selfhood involves no others. In concluding that this is a matter of choice or opinion, we run counter to the structures of observable reality.

If we ask ourselves why it is that we are concerned about our uniqueness, or the uniqueness of another existent, don't we have to reply that it is because we wish to understand what it means to be *self*-conscious of the fact that we exist in encounters of otherness? We seek to justify our lives, our actions and thoughts, because we know that there are others to whom we are related, with whom we compare, and must forever be responsible. Justification is the struggle to acquire a certain legitimacy in relation to the others who share existence with us. The others may be friends, employers, God, or true Self (as in the atman-Brahman dialectic of India).

Religious systems and philosophies emerge as expressions of our participation in these dramas with the need for justification, identity, and understanding. The entire human enterprise bustles with its ideas, manipulations, and struggles because we must contend with the fact that every phase of our existence tells a story of the self among others. How to manage balancing the singular other with the fact that he is also representative other is our assignment. It is why we are concerned with issues of inferiority and superiority, uniqueness and similarity, why we must be able to have some justification for our thoughts and actions. It is why we are religious above all else—whether that religiousness expresses itself in traditional forms or not.

Melville has something to say of this at the beginning of chapter forty-six of *Moby Dick*:

> Though, consumed with the hot fire of his purpose, Ahab in all his thoughts and actions ever had in view the ultimate capture of Moby Dick; though he seemed ready to sacrifice all mortal interests to that one passion; nevertheless it may have been that he was by nature and long habituation far too wedded to a fiery whaleman's ways, altogether to abandon the collateral prosecution of the voyage. Or at least if this were otherwise, there were not wanting other motives much more influential with him. It would be refining too much, perhaps, even considering his monomania, to hint that his vindictiveness towards the White Whale might have possibly extended itself in some degree to all sperm whales, and that the more monsters he slew by so much the more he multiplied the chances that each subsequently encountered whale would prove to be the hated one he hunted.[5]

When, for whatever reason, the other is so much the one who threatens us, it is rather easy for us to extend our fears and hatred to the representative others who share similar characteristics. Our rage against otherness is directed to "all sperm whales" in the hope that we may slay the singular white whale who is the cause of our anxiety.

It should be evident that the representative other is encountered in the same roles as the singular other. However we observe or experience the other as representative of some group, we know these others as benefactor, malefactor, mystery, and power. Ahab is the slayer of all monsters of the deep because he was the victim of some instinctive cruelty by one of those sperm whales. The mystery and the power of the White Whale took the form of malefactor for Ahab, and he was un-

---

[5]Herman Melville, *Moby Dick* (New York: The Modern Library, 1950) 211.

able to dissociate this singular other from its representative relationship to the many other sperm whales.

This conflation is the key to all sorts of prejudicial and erratic behavior. It must be understood that behind our discriminatory acts and often violent slayings of all "sperm whales" is an important and essential truth: we are never absolutely autonomous beings. Even as singular other, we are singular only with regard to our relationship to an other; furthermore, the relationship is such that we share characteristics of otherness that make us representative. I am a human male. I cannot disregard the fact that the maleness makes me representative. I cannot idealistically claim to be just a singular, autonomous being, for such is false and unrealistic. Even to claim that I am "merely" a human being means that I am asserting my otherness in representative fashion and in relationship to other beings. It is the fact that singular and representative otherness exist in dialectical engagement in our experience that makes abuse possible. The law is necessary, because without it, our tendency to see all sperm whales as Moby Dick would make for chaotic existence.

It should not be necessary to point out that the tension discussed here is productive of goodness as well as evil or harm. The fact that you are representative as well as singular may mean that I accept your worth because I assume in advance that you are worthy. If I know that you are a physician, I expect that you will perform as benefactor, as a dispenser of benevolent power. Yet as a singular other, you may not be at all worthy of my assumption and trust. Quite simply, existence does not permit the luxury of testing in advance, or even in depth, the worth of each singular other. We can only live with certain assumptions and expectations, reserving the extent of our response until there is evidence of either benefactor or malefactor.

The behavior that results from the tension between the singular other and the representative other is not exclusively observed in others. It is behavior that we ourselves demonstrate. If I am a Japanese Buddhist, there will be distinctive forms of behavior that I assume as part of my representative otherness, while at the same time I may claim for myself certain personal adaptations. However, even this does not escape the representative character of otherness; rather, it simply demonstrates its dialectical relation to our singularity. In sum, we all to a certain extent behave as representatives.

Criminals frequently identify with the representative character of their selfhood. They accept the role of malefactor and begin to behave knowingly as a representative. Recently, in Arizona, someone tried to stay the execution of a convicted murderer. He had been involved in violent crime a number of times, both inside and outside the prison. The prisoner himself opposed the delay of his death penalty: "Hey! I know what kind of person I am. And I'm not gonna change. If I got out of here right now, I'd probably kill somebody. It don't mean nothin' to me. So okay, I'm ready to take what's comin' to me. Don't cheat me out of it!" Is it possible that much of the aberration and mental disorder of our society stems from a failure to maintain proper tension between the singular and the representative in the encounters of otherness? As a murderer, the individual has permitted his singularity to be sufficient unto itself. This is an impossibility, however, since one is always related to others. At the same time, a representative otherness denoted by such terms as murderer and criminal has so identified itself with his singularity that his freedom to be both singular and representative is lost.

It is good for me to know that I belong to others, that I can accept a certain categorization that suggests that I am never absolutely alone. I am part of the otherness that is my profession. I am also part of the institution and community that make my profession workable. There is a sense of belonging to a family, and also perhaps to a racial or ethnic group. It may be that I have traditional religious identity, along with a sense of being American. With all of this representative otherness, there is a peculiar singularity that keeps the representative from smothering that aspect of the otherness of existence that remains open possibility, sheer potential. Of course, I am faithful to the representative character of otherness, since that is a fundamental way in which the freedom-to-be-other asserts itself. After all, it is as a child of Israel that I have come to know that I am more than what is shared with me by the otherness of the earth and its vitalities. I become a child of the covenant. I represent it; it represents me. I have a singular and unique responsibility because I have shared this insight and meaning. Indeed, I can only measure the course of my singular human responsibility by reference to my representative relationship to Israel and the covenant.

The categories of representative otherness are numerous and varied. It is hardly necessary to spend much time on detailed description of them. A social-scientific account of representative otherness would probably achieve that more satisfactorily. I have already mentioned some of the possibilities in the preceding paragraph. Nicolas Berdyaev speaks of nationalism as an idolatrous outgrowth of nationality, "a product of modern history which has lost its sense of unity and is moving toward particularism." Nationalism is thus another form of fusion, whereby the singular identifies itself with the representative. Nationality, however, may be another matter. "It must be admitted that Nationalism, as one of the degrees of the individualization of being, has undoubted and positive value. Culture always had national character and roots. An international culture is impossible. Only technics are truly international and they have a strong internationalizing influence. Nationalism is a cultural and historic fact. It is an attitude toward facts, but it transforms a natural fact into an idol."[6] For Berdyaev, nationality is a category of what I have called representative otherness. It is a broad category of peoplehood, indicating the interdependency of human reality on a scale that extends beyond family and identifies itself with territory. Some awareness of and responsible attention to nationality seems inevitable. However, when nationality becomes the occasion wherein we lose sight of the unity in persons that exists due to the interplay of singular and representative otherness, then it becomes a false singularity, what Berdyaev calls particularism. It becomes nationalism and makes inordinate claims for itself, demanding the absolute loyalty and reverence of those who are part of it. It faces all others with the same demands and expectations.

Nationality differs from race and ethnicity in that biological or linguistic factors are essential ingredients in the latter two. Of course, race or ethnicity may also become nationality, but they do not *necessarily* assume that identity. When I observe a black man, I am aware of the fact that he is a representative of a race of people. On initial encounter, I have no idea whether he is American, African, West Indian. His race is apparent for biological reasons, but his nationality is not. If he is African, he probably originates from any one of a number of

---

[6]Nicolas Berdyaev, *The Fate of Man in the Modern World* (Ann Arbor: The University of Michigan Press, 1969) 88.

tribal, ethnic, and national traditions. I encounter him as a representative other (as he does me), but I must remember that his representative character is not limited to what I see. He is also the embodiment of a singular otherness that must be honored. He cannot escape certain aspects of his representative otherness, but he should not be reduced to those particularities.

"The fate of man," writes Berdyaev, "is infinitely more complex than it was thought to be in the nineteenth century. The new world which is taking form is moved by other values than the value of man or of human personality, or the value of truth: it is moved by such values as power, technics, race-purity, nationality, the state, the class, the collective. The will to justice is overcome by the will to power."[7] Berdyaev's philosophizing succeeds dramatically in demonstrating for us the human characteristic of sharing existence with a variety of representative others. Some form of society is inescapable. Some means of expressing our relationship to various forms of power, mystery, benevolence, and malevolence is essential for us. The dehumanization Berdyaev deplores is the outcome of our lack of vision in these matters. In the twentieth century we have lost our sight: we do not *see* that our humanity is always more than the social order that wishes to encompass us, the technocratic civilization that cleverly convinces us that its form of power is total and comprehensive.

"Society," writes Talcott Parsons, "is a religiously based moral order characterized by congruence between the cultural, structural, and personality levels of the social system."[8] "Cultural, structural, and personality levels" allude to the fact that we become aware of ourselves as a people in the midst of multiple sets of representative otherness. The manner in which that awareness finds clarification will be descriptive of the type of society and culture. Societies, institutions, organizations, voluntary associations—all these express the essential otherness of existence. Technology and the process of dehumanization are dominant features in the forms of representative otherness that are peculiar to our society. Their presence may result in a closure

---

[7]Ibid., 29.

[8]For a clear formulation of Parsons's view, see Richard K. Fenn, "The Process of Secularization: A Post-Parsonsian View," *Journal for the Scientific Study of Religion* 9 (1970): 119.

of what is distinctively human. If we have created a world that merely functions, however well, we will have somehow escaped the otherness of being. We will be party to no other, we will simply belong to a pattern of causation. Yet in spite of all this, our present society is simply a form of our human need to deal with the various others that are part of the encounters of existence. If we retain the vision of life that preserves the tension between singular and representative otherness, dehumanization cannot take place. Freedom is this vision: it is the ability to acknowledge the otherness that is constant to our selfhood and to all of reality. It is the basis of religion and of its study.

In addition to the varieties of social expression of otherness, there emerges another expression equally important for the study of religion: tradition. Tradition is the lore, the transmitted (oral and written) experience, the teachings and practices that seek to be faithful to responsible awareness of the encounters of otherness. It is the persistence of tradition that provides continuity and renewal to religion. Gershom Scholem, discussing religious authority and mysticism, remarks: "From a historical point of view, the mystical quest for the divine takes place almost exclusively within a prescribed tradition—the exceptions seem to be limited to modern times, with their dissolution of all traditional ties."[9] One hardly knows how to approach the statement. Has it been the absence of traditional ties that accounts for the clumsy deflowering of the mystical quest? Or is it that the narcissism of our modern quest has rendered impotent the great traditions?

One thing seems certain: if a sane society depends upon its sensitivity to the otherness of existence, its vision that our humanity is always more than its successes and failures, then there must be something to preserve and nourish that sensitivity and vision. Tradition remembers the appearance of such vision and sensitivity, and serves as custodian of its secrets and teacher of its arts of realization. A society devoid of traditional ties has no means for nourishing the most obvious and essential fact of existence—its character as encountering otherness.

Religions have been the most prevalent representatives of such tradition. They are not alone, of course, because our basic human re-

---

[9] Gershom Scholem, *On the Kabbalah and Its Symbolism* (New York: Schocken Books, 1965, 1977) 5-6.

ligiousness finds many forms of expression. There is a scientific tradition that also nourishes the vision of otherness. One can see it in the lives of Einstein, Jung, Heisenberg, and Eiseley. But the scientific vision is receding also. Science, too, has begun to witness the dissolution of its traditional ties in a vulgar narcissistic struggle to patch, to solve, to produce. It also has been victimized by power.

Tradition is formed not just to preserve and promote the vision. It exists to *represent* the vision in a particular way. It exists as a matter of identity, and as an acknowledgment of the fact that although the singular other gains certain insights, she or he gains them as a creature among others, as a result of others. Further, the manner in which the story of these insights is told makes that person a representative other. Scholem says that the moment the person

> tries to clarify his experience by reflection, to formulate it, and especially when he attempts to communicate it to others, he cannot help imposing a framework of conventional symbols and ideas upon it. To be sure, there is always some part of it that he cannot adequately and fully express. But if he does try to communicate his experience—and it is only by doing so that he makes himself known to us—he is bound to interpret his experience in a language, in images and concepts, that were created before him.[10]

It is as a representative other that we nourish and communicate the vision of otherness. What the vision itself communicates is our representative relationship to the whole of being. Tradition, as the cluster of images, concepts, language, is the embodiment of the sensitivity and vision of otherness.

We are very likely to bear tradition in a distinctive way. We shall be Muslim, Christian, Jew, or Buddhist. Even if we find ourselves somewhat removed or alienated from the institutional forms of a tradition, we find it informing our thinking or serving as a contextual factor in the creation of our systems. Our thoughts and actions are so much a part of the encounters of otherness that they are always in some sense representative. As we become aware of the fact that tradition is the custodian of vision and understanding, we may discover our identity as a representative of a *particular* tradition.

---

[10]Ibid., 8.

Tradition recognizes the truth that the otherness of existence is not static. It is always in process, in motion. Just as space is an arrangement of motions that reflects the fluidity of otherness, so time is the measure of our own participation in the arrangements of motion. Tradition is our vision and reflection upon the meaning of that participation. John Meyendorff speaks traditionally when he says that "tradition is the sacramental continuity in history of the communion of saints."[11] He points to the manner in which the truth of existence is mediated to us by its own moving light. Tradition holds a special knowledge, a special memory, in the midst of whatever ordinary understanding we have of the motional character of existence. This latter understanding is the gift of science. Again, speaking as a traditional Christian (in the most positive sense of that adjective), Meyendorff writes:

> Knowledge of Christ and communion with God (that which was called theosis by the Fathers) are not communicated to men so that they may in any way *replace* man's knowledge of himself and of the cosmos, but in order to fulfill that knowledge, to give it a new meaning and a new creative dimension. Thus, the knowledge which comes from revelation, from Scripture and from Tradition, does not replace culture and science, but liberates the human mind from the secular or a-religious, i.e. from a necessarily one-sided approach to the reality of man and to the world.[12]

Tradition possesses a liberating knowledge of our continuity among the others who make up reality with us. Without that vision, that knowledge, we are the prisoners of a passionless determinism.

Tradition is a source of authority. By it we know who we are and whence we have come. We know our story. Tradition provides us with the beginning and sense of ending for our story. It offers us the "once upon a time"—the source, the author—a recollection of the fact that we have come from others, and are part of others as they are part of us. It also reminds us that we must go on performing the liberating task of telling the story. The story is of our own telling, but it is a story

---

[11]John Meyendorff, *Living Tradition* (Crestwood: St. Vladimir's Seminary Press, 1978) 16.

[12]Ibid., 93.

that began "once upon a time" and will end with another "once upon a time." We have a certain role to play in the story and we must do it well, tell it well, yet it *is* a role. We are always representative others as well as singular others and the real liberation is in the *telling* of what happened between one and the other, between the self and the dramas of otherness of which we are a part.

John Meyendorff, discussing the problem of authority in religion, refers to the work of the nineteenth-century Russian lay theologian, A. S. Khomiakov. The latter held that in the West, "authority became external power." Church authority vested knowledge of religious truths in human *reason* alone, and set itself up as an external guardian of what was necessary for salvation. "And in the Reformation the external authority of the Church was replaced by that of Scripture." In both cases, the authority is some external source—pope or Bible. But, says Khomiakov, in the Orthodox East there is not really a concern for authority at all.

> The Church is not an authority, just as God is not an authority, since authority is something external to us. The Church is not authority, I say, but the Truth—and at the same time the inner life of the Christian, since God, Christ, the Church live in him with a life more real than the heart which is beating in his breast and the blood flowing in his veins.[13]

Khomiakov really points to a different view of authority itself. After all, there must be authority. The issue of authority is ever inescapable. It involves the question, What is the *source* and foundation of what I think, believe and do? The Russian theologian was suggesting that Orthodoxy's understanding of authority relies upon the manner in which truth incarnates itself, through tradition, in the lives of human beings. I think it is not inappropriate to maintain that authority is always dependent upon the correlation between tradition as the story of the vision of otherness and the individual as storyteller. It is not wholly an external matter nor is it entirely internal. Each of us must be able to rely upon the story we tell; but it is only the telling that brings the truth into living encounter.

---

[13]Ibid., 27.

Tradition becomes living intellect in the course of its embodiment as truth, for it can only exist as that which takes place between humans. It exists fleetingly as the perception that brings clarity to the experience of being a one among others, an other among various forms of singular and representative others. Tradition is like a dream, existing but a brief moment, yet spanning a whole episode in the chapters of our unconscious life of fancy and anxiety. This kind of dream is a political necessity, however. In order to live as human beings, protecting the rights and responsibilities of our singular and representative otherness, we need the dream, the story, that tells the deep truth about us.

Tradition helps us to live in the city of humanity. I live with others, working out the necessities of our togetherness by way of a story that tells each of us who we are. My dream may be Buddhist, while yours is Christian or Navajo. The fact that we have different stories does not mean that we are separate, removed from each other. For we are not only representative others as Buddhists and Navajos, we are also racial, ethnic, and national. We are also representative of humanity in relationship to animals; and we are representative of living beings as distinct from inorganic reality. It is precisely this wide degree of representation that reminds us that both we and the other are also singular in our otherness.

In telling our story, it becomes truth. At this point it is not Buddhist truth or Christian truth, but truth. There is no appropriate adjective for truth that has other than external authority. At the moment of incarnation, it has become internal, though not *contained* by us. We cannot avoid the external manner in which tradition claims us as its representative, but we also cannot avoid the fact that it is truth itself that is presented to us and in us.

IV / The Contours
of Otherness:
The Wholly Other

*He was my friend. We went through the war together. He did not return.
So it is up to us to will his presence here, amongst us. Though the others
did not know him, couldn't have known him, they will bear witness for
him and in his place.*

*He did not resemble them? So what! Each of them has experienced
more than one life and suffered more than one torment, visited many a
country, obeyed certain laws and transgressed many others. Each
knows the secret is eternal and eternally hidden. The roads lead no-
where, they converge not at one but at a thousand points. He who says
"I" has said everything. Just as every man contains all men, this word
contains all words. It is the only word God uttered at Mount Sinai. Yet
one must know how to pronounce it as He does. He says "I" and it
means: I who am with you, within you. We say "I" and it means: I who
am opposed to you, all of you. His "I" embraces all men, ours divides
them. On His lips "I" means love, on ours too, but it is no longer the
same love. For it is easy for us to love one another, it is even easy to love
our enemies: much easier than to love ourselves.*[1]

In these words from *A Beggar in Jerusalem*, Elie Wiesel
expresses a significant fact about the contours of otherness. What we
perceive are the shapes and contours of a reality that shares itself with

---

[1]Elie Wiesel, *A Beggar in Jerusalem* (New York: Random House, 1970) 7.

every other, while at the same time reserving a wholeness beyond all individual manifestations. "Just as every man contains all men, this word ["I"] contains all words." To be of a mind to say "I" is to transcend in a measure that reality of which one is a part and of which one is speaking. We are other to that otherness we share with every person. If we disregard the "I" of our transcendence, we have lapsed into the primordial chaos that preceded creation. However, if we take that "I" to mean that, in our singular and representative otherness, we are superior to all that is real around us and that we must subdue it, then we have frustrated the dynamic character of otherness. There is an otherness to "I" that makes it *ultimately* other, *wholly* other. "We say 'I' and it means: I who am opposed to you, all of you. His 'I' embraces all men, ours divides them."

This is the crux of what H. Richard Niebuhr tells us in his *Radical Monotheism and Western Culture.* "Radical monotheism dethrones all absolutes short of the principle of being itself. At the same time it reverences every relative existent."[2] In other words, radical monotheism (to use Niebuhr's terms) says: "I" am other than what you call the realms and workings of nature; "I" am other than the neighbor who is near you in the "passing association" of your interest group; "I" am other than the neighbor in your church, your race, your nation; "I" am other than the one who is mirrored in your visions of selfhood. "I" am all of these things and more. "I" am the one beyond all the many. "I" am in them and they in me. "Monotheism is less than radical if it makes a distinction between the principle of being and the principle of value; so that while all being is acknowledged as absolutely dependent for existence on the One, only some beings are valued as having worth for it."[3]

It is appropriate to further explain what is meant by "wholly other." Often the emphasis appears to be, as it is for many absolute monotheists, directed toward a separate being who is *entirely* other, absolutely other. Certainly there are moments in our experience when we may be aware of that awesome and tremendous "Other" who stands over against us, as theologians Rudolf Otto and Karl Barth speak of it. For

---

[2]H. Richard Niebuhr, *Radical Monotheism and Western Culture* (New York: Harper & Brothers, 1960) 37.

[3]Ibid., 32.

Mole and Water Rat in *The Wind in the Willows*, there was great awe before some august presence as they searched among the willows looking for Baby Otter. Mole dared to risk, to raise his eyes.

> He might not refuse, were Death himself waiting to strike him instantly, once he had looked with mortal eye on things rightly kept hidden. And then he looked, trembling, into the very eyes of the awesome Being. "Rat!" he said to his friend in a whisper, "Are you afraid?" "Afraid?" murmured the Rat, his eyes shining with unutterable love. "Afraid! Of Him? Oh, never, never! And yet—and yet—Oh, Mole, I am afraid!" Then the two animals, crouching to the earth bowed their heads and did worship.

Yet even this experience should not be interpreted as an encounter with that which is entirely or *absolutely* other. It is only possible to maintain such a distinction in a very formalistic manner, and only if we suppose that there is no continuity whatsoever in the experience of reality. However, if we assert some absolute discontinuity between ourselves and a wholly other, the very fact of our assertion establishes that there is sufficient continuity to make the observation.

It should be clear by now that the nature of otherness requires a dialectical understanding. Even a *wholly* other is other *to us*, and we to it. Is it not better, therefore, to think of the other as a whole of which we are a part, yet, because of this awareness we may still stand in freedom? This is a whole that is more than the sum of its parts. This other is the whole beyond the many, whence all singular and representative others derive their being, and by participation in which they exist. We must learn to trust the whole of otherness for the significance of *our* selfhood and *all else* that shares the otherness of being. This is what the New Testament maintains when it reminds us that "in Him we live and move and have our being."

Eastern Orthodox theology, among all the theologies of the Christian tradition, expresses this thought most provocatively and insistently. This theology maintains that the Christian revelation does not begin with rationalistic assumptions about the nature of God, but affirms "the irreducible ultimacy of a *personal* God, at once absolute *and* personal." In other words, it does more than affirm the absolute otherness of God; it insists that mankind has access to this otherness and can know it. It is not some metaphysical monotheism that requires the dissolution of the person as a means of relationship. Nor is it monotheistic *obedience* to a personal being without insight into, and participation *in*, the divine nature.

> Revelation is thus a "theocosmic" relationship which includes us. Not only can we not know God outside it, but we cannot judge it "objectively" from outside. Revelation knows of no "outside," for it *is* this relationship between God and the World within which, like it or not, we find ourselves. But in the immanence of revelation, God affirms Himself to be transcendent to creation. . . . Pure transcendence is impossible: if one conceives God as the transcendent cause of the universe, He cannot be purely transcendent since the very idea of a cause implies that of effect. In the dialectic of revelation, immanence allows us to name transcendence. But there would be no immanence whatsoever if transcendence were not, in its depth, inaccessible. That is why we cannot think of God in Himself, in His essence.[4]

Of course, this essay is not concerned with the vindication of Christianity or any form of Christian thought. But it is interesting to reflect on the manner in which Eastern Christian thinking assists in a discussion of the wholly other as the wholeness I have been describing. It would seem that existence as the encounter of otherness requires a study of the wholly other as part of the study of religion. Simply put, the wholly other is fundamental to the comprehension of every religious phenomenon one may analyze. Moreover, it is fundamental to the study of all phenomena—whether political, natural, or social. Any form of observation and analysis is a transcendent action. We find ourselves set apart from what is other to us, yet not entirely so. As scientists we may classify certain others as representative, but we must also treat them singularly. Further, in our conscious acts of observation or manipulation, we affect the results of our own efforts, often intentionally. What we study includes ourselves and our transcendent actions. As others we are always more than our momentary formations and conscious acts. We are participants in a wholly other, which includes us—in which we live and move and have our being. The wholly other is a participant in every human act and is, then, an ingredient in what we study. The wholly other is a legitimate item for

---

[4]Vladimir Lossky, *Orthodox Theology: An Introduction* (Crestwood: St. Vladimir's Seminary Press, 1978) 31.

our studies. It is generally ignored, of course. We are afraid of it and may rage against it, as Ahab did. What we must continue to attempt is find a way to gain knowledge and understanding that does justice to the living reality of the wholly other.

In his autobiography, Loren Eiseley writes of some giant wasps of the genus *Sphecius*. He muses on the effect of the coming of the great wasps with their boundless energy, their paralyzing power. They frighten people. Through his encounter with them, Eiseley first began to doubt what he calls "the naturalness of nature." "The great wasps, the invaders of the autumn grass, carry navigational aids whose complexity is unexplained and whose surgical intent is comprehended, if at all, only in the dream that lies below all living nature. . . . I have come to believe that in the world there is nothing to explain the world. Nothing in nature that can separate the existent from the potential."[5] In a sense, Eiseley is too modest. In his remarks, he *is* explaining the world. That is the only explanation possible. We humans commit transcendent acts. We are *in* the world, yet in transcendent actions we explain the reality of which we are a part. The world of nature is other to us and we to it. We have explained it by calling it "nature." Nevertheless, our transcendent otherness points beyond itself to an other of which it is only a part. Therefore, our explanations are centered in continuing mystery. "My thoughts are not your thoughts," writes Eiseley, quoting the biblical precept. It is almost impossible, he says, to explain the peculiar knowledge of the Sphex wasps. Natural selection has a difficult time of it.

> I am an evolutionist. I believe my great backyard Sphexes have evolved like other creatures. But watching them in the October light as one circles my head in curiosity, I can only repeat my dictum softly: in the world there is nothing to explain the world. Nothing to explain the necessity of life, nothing to explain the hunger of the elements to become life. . . . On that lovely backyard slope it had somehow pleased me that the wasps came and went as though I belonged to another world they chose to ignore, a misty world for which they carried no instruction, *just as I carried none for the totality of the night*. Though shorn of knowledge, willing to *accept the dreadful otherness* of the Biblical challenge, "your ways are not my ways," I had come to feel at last that the

---

[5]Loren Eiseley, *All the Strange Hours* (New York: Charles Scribner's Sons, 1975) 238.

human version of evolutionary events was perhaps too simplistic for belief.[6]

We are evolutionists, because in our transcendent observation of that otherness to which we belong, we become aware of continuity, of relationship. But our observation is part of what we observe. There is a *"dreadful* otherness" to it all, an awesome otherness that is wholly other, that makes our premature and absolutist conclusions about what we observed "too simplistic for belief." The wholly other—that which says, "your thoughts are not my thoughts, your ways are not my ways"—is a legitimate reality for study because it is manifest in everything we do. To approach religion without an awareness, a struggle to understand the wholly other, is not to study religion. The same is naturally true of other intellectual and scholarly pursuits. As Eiseley shows us, the act of hypothesizing and theorizing is a participation in transcendent otherness. Martin Buber invoked this theme by saying that

> in every sphere, through everything that becomes present to us, we gaze toward the train of the eternal You; in each we perceive a breath of it; in every You we address the eternal You, in every sphere according to its manner.[7]

What Buber and others reveal to us is a very ordinary fact of existence: that there is creative flow to reality, that the varieties of consciousness (that which becomes present to us) are participants in an eternal You, a Wholly Other, which is more than the sum of its parts. To conceive of a singular other in some totally insular manner is an impossibility. Whether the singular other is a person, place, thing, or *a* Supreme Being or God, does not matter. The singular other exists in relationship to others of both singular and representative nature, yet the otherness is not exhausted. It continues to transcend, to be of a whole. The eternal You, the wholly other, is present in all spheres of consciousness, in each "according to its manner."

All attempts to limit otherness are arbitrary. They are forms of individualism and particularism. Only an understanding of personality

---

⁶Ibid., 242.

⁷Martin Buber, *I and Thou* (New York: Charles Scribner's Sons, 1970) 57.

provides an appropriate basis for a consideration of reality. This is because the wholly other is party to all circumstances of reality. What
the physical and social sciences ordinarily do is construct for us a
creature called human, which is actually the offspring of the world and
its need to limit and restrict. We build robots and computers in order
to alleviate drudgery and simplify the living of our days. Much of what
results, of course, fuels the assumption that proper functioning makes
for qualitative existence. It is an easy matter to transfer those same
assumptions to speculation and decision about our own nature. We
fail to discern a certain freedom about our existence. We are like nothing else around us, yet related to all things and to all being.

By "nature" we are individuals in a scheme emerging out of our
rage for order, because "nature" is of our own construction. However,
we are not nature; we are personality. "Personality," writes Berdyaev,
"is a microcosm, a complete universe. It is personality alone that can
bring together a universal content and be a potential universe."[8] Since
it is a microcosm, it is not an individual piece of something larger: personality is the whole of reality. All others are part of personality. Personality is the wholly other; it is always the exception to the law, always
the *more than* in the very midst of our thought, our consciousness, our
actions. "Personality is not a biological or a psychological category,
but an ethical and spiritual [category]."[9] The worth of our humanity
does not reside in biological or psychological content, but in the fact
that we are free to do and to be *more than*. Our freedom to do is the
root of our ethical nature; our freedom to be *more than* is the heart of
our spirituality.

It should be obvious that as individuals we cannot lay *claim* to the
wholly other that is the microcosm of our personality. We cannot identify ourselves or any other singular or representative other as the
whole which our otherness reflects. We cannot call ourselves or any
other "God." God is the *more than* that is in our midst. God is the macrocosm, of which we are microcosm. God, too, as wholly other, is personality. The wholly other is, therefore, not known as some grand
object whose existence we may discover if we search diligently. The

---

[8]Nicolas Berdyaev, *Slavery and Freedom* (New York: Charles Scribner's Sons, 1944)
21.

[9]Ibid., 25.

wholly other is not to be defined as an architect or first cause, the existence of which we can either admit to or not according to desire or inclination. The wholly other is known, not defined. We know God as the freedom to be and to do. We know God in the struggle, the suffering, and the pain that go along with the process of achieving the freedom that is our personality. There is suffering, even crucifixion, in the attempt to close off the constant interplay of otherness that forms our personality. There is the temptation to declare our individuality as sufficient unto itself, to deny the wholly other that is in our midst. "God," says Berdyaev, "is the guarantee of the freedom of personality from the enslaving power of nature and society, of the kingdom of Caesar and of the object world."[10]

Since the issue of the relationship of the wholly other to the name of God has been raised, perhaps it would be useful to take the discussion a bit further. The point is that the namers of God have not all been infantile believers who posit the existence of a being whom intelligent humans cannot countenance and whose presence cannot be tolerated in the halls of academe. What the intelligent namers of God speak of is a reality that is like ourselves—inasmuch as we are microcosm.

In the writings of the Anglican theologian Austin Farrer, there is a discussion of Thomas Altizer's *The Gospel of Christian Atheism*.[11] Farrer speaks of Altizer's reaction against the notion of God as Byzantine emperor. In struggling to understand Altizer without recourse to a "sort of metaphysical rant," Farrer says: "The act of condescension by which God serves his creatures in making them make themselves is no self-annihilation on God's part, it is simply the appropriate use of his power: *it is the only way to make such a world as this is*." Farrer goes on to say that Altizer is overscrupulously concerned that we be "saved from a crushing transcendence by the singular act of God himself."[12] Those who have no time or thought for including God in the academic study of religion are likely to be among those who are tired of crushing and irrelevant transcendence. They are certain that transcendence cannot be dealt with in the realms of empirical observation.

---

[10]Ibid., 27.

[11]Austin Farrer, *Reflective Faith* (Grand Rapids: Eerdmans, 1974) 175-76.

[12]Ibid., 175-77.

What if the transcendence is that in which we live and move and have our being? What if the transcendent is not a Byzantine emperor? If human beings are personalities, they are the microcosm of a wholly other. There is then no consciousness, no thought, no action not involved in an otherness that is inexhaustible even though it is constantly giving of its wholeness. Farrer believes that when Altizer writes of God's death, he cannot mean "that God got hanged one Friday about the year 30 and that was that. He must mean that the Crucifixion was a decisive, a revealing point *in a continuous action of God*, who is constantly dying to himself that he may be reborn in the life and action of his creatures."[13] If this is the meaning behind the naming of God, then God is wholly other, and not a luxury to the process of study and investigation. God is both investigator and investigated.

"But theologians will cry out in alarm that Jesus Christ alone was God-man, and that man is a created being and cannot be God-man. Such an argument remains within the confines of theological rationalism."[14] Therein is expressed the objection that many theologians and believers may bring against the interpretation of the wholly other that I have been using. These objections are concerned with the protection of some particularistic rational scheme. They represent those who are dedicated more to the preservation of private property than to the sharing of personal truth. Within the Eastern Orthodox tradition, there are concepts and practices that transcend such rationalism. The ideas of deification and theosis discovered there suggest that human personality is a field in which otherness is at work. The singular and representative otherness always shares in the wholly other and in some ways manifests that wholly otherness. To those Christians who worry about Jesus Christ's uniqueness, the East says with Robert Browning, " 'Man partly is and *wholly* hopes to be.' But to discern the potentialities inherent in man, one must regard him from the point of view of the revelation in Christ."[15]

---

[13]Ibid., 176.

[14]Matthew Spinka, *Nicolas Berdyaev: Captive of Freedom* (Philadelphia: The Westminster Press, 1950) 144.

[15]Ibid., 138.

The Christ that is known, in Eastern thought, is the *risen* Christ. It is, therefore, a Christ known today. It is a risen Christ who is met in liturgy and the Eucharist, a risen Christ who introduces the Scriptures and tells the truth of their teaching. Orthodoxy is a tradition that focuses on the personal. The personal is always the encounter and experience of otherness. "The true greatness of man," writes Vladimir Lossky, "is not in his incontestable kinship with the universe, but in his participation in divine plenitude, in the mystery within himself of the 'image' and the 'likeness.' "[16] The divine plenitude is the whole of otherness that is shared; the knowledge of this is always by way of the risen Christ—a knowledge that offers a vision of wholeness that is itself personal. We are the image and likeness of God, who is wholly other.

John Dewey is an American philosopher who could teach religion scholars a great deal. Not that he provides a satisfactory "system." That is an impossible task. However, in his quest for a system, he was surprised by insights that can be helpful. For Dewey, human religiousness is a virtual given. It is essential and inescapable. The question is, What do we do with this religiousness? The wrong thing to do, according to Dewey, is to feed it to religions and permit religions to devour it. It is certainly true that religion frequently (perhaps most often) becomes the palace of Altizer's Byzantine emperor, circumscribing the dynamism of personality and confining our religiousness in unnatural ways. What Dewey did not wish to understand is that religion also carries in its tradition the special vision that transforms pedestrian nature into liberated personality. Religion is always both the result of our religiousness and the sustainer of it. This is true even though the realms of religiousness are not confined to religions.

The contemporary religious problem, according to Dewey, is the integration of our modern beliefs about the world with our convictions about what is most worthy and purposive human behavior.

> Within the flickering inconsequential acts of separate selves dwells a sense of the whole which claims and dignifies them. In its presence we put off mortality and live in the universal. The life of the community in which we live and have our being is the fit symbol of this relation-

---

[16]Lossky, *Orthodox Theology*, 70.

ship. The acts in which we express our perception of the ties which bind us to others are its only rites and ceremonies.[17]

Dewey's vision of the whole is an interesting one, especially for our purposes. One gets the feeling, however, that Dewey's sense of the whole is of an "all" that comprises the addition of all those "separate selves" he notes. He seems not to be sufficiently aware of selfhood as a complex multiplicity of encounters with otherness which, as a *whole*, is itself other to, and greater than, the sum of its parts. We who observe these goings-on, and recognize our participation in them, know how they evade definition. In short, we know that we are personality, that the whole is itself personality, and that there is no other way of describing it.

Dewey, of course, as a good Puritan, wishes to confine the whole to morality and community. The only valid rite and ceremony are moral acts; and moral acts are done for the benefit of the whole, which in Dewey's understanding is a community—an "all" as the sum of its parts. The manner in which otherness always points beyond any closure, to a whole that is being itself, is of little or no interest to him. However, I have argued that community is a worthy concept only if it points beyond life to a sense of unity and purpose with the whole of being. Dewey, though, is not entirely insensitive to this problem. In *A Common Faith*, he writes of the idea of the whole as an "imaginative, not a literal, idea. . . . The whole self is an ideal, an imaginative projection." He comes close to the notion of the wholly other when he admits that the composing of the self in harmony with the universe "is not voluntary in the sense of an act of special volition or resolution."[18] Such an effect is expressive of *will*, says Dewey, yet is not its express product. Here he certainly recognizes that he is dealing with a reality that is not a matter of mechanical cause and effect. It would seem that it is also more than an ideal, since an ideal is something usually utilized as a tool in the attempt to accomplish certain ends.

It is pertinent to note that the composing of the self throughout the ceaseless flux of what it does, suffers, and achieves, cannot be at-

---

[17]John Dewey, *Human Nature and Conduct* (New York: Henry Holt and Company, 1922) 331-32.

[18]John Dewey, *A Common Faith* (New Haven: Yale University Press, 1934) 19.

tained in terms of itself. The self is always directed toward something
beyond itself and so its own unification depends upon the idea of the
integration of the shifting scenes of the world into that imaginative totality we call the Universe.[19]

Taken by itself, this statement seems in harmony with an understanding of otherness as participation in a wholly other. But Dewey remains
too apprehensive about the ("crushing"?) transcendent character of
the "something beyond itself." Hence, his "imaginative totality" is
pulled back into "the power of an ideal"—a workable instrument.

The wholly other is always more than ideal, and more than community—in Dewey's sense of it. Indeed, that is the mark of its wholeness. Additionally, the fact that it is otherness that is being discussed
makes it a very concrete reality, for an other can never be abstract.
Whatever stands in relationship to us is concrete; it sets the stage on
which human consciousness and thought are formed. As an imaginative totality, the wholly other is more than *ignis fatuus*. The imagining
of totality is a substantial event. It is derived from the discovery that
every tree, animal, person, and idea offers relation to the wholly other.
Transcendence is not an option or a possibility; it is a presence.

Otherness is singular, representative, and whole. What has been
said of the singular and representative other is also true of the wholly
other. It is known in degrees of insight and it is known as benefactor,
malefactor, mystery, and power. It is because we encounter the wholly
other in every meeting with singular and representative other that we
frequently find it convenient to *identify* what we have encountered *with*
the wholly other. In traditional religion this form of identification is
known as idolatry. The idol is not always the object of idolatrous affairs, though. When we perceive transcendence as something of
beauty, mystery, and power, we may wish to retain the image of that
embodiment. We recognize the wholly other and may wish to honor it
and keep it. An idol or an icon may be the result. However, it is not necessarily true that we worship the image as if it were the wholly other.
We also have the gift of transparent sight, which sees through the image to the *more than* in the midst of it. Since that is how our perception
of reality takes place, it stands to reason that everything we see is an
image of the wholly other and susceptible to idolization.

---

[19]Ibid.

Often the most intelligent of us tend to be dualists. We assume the superiority of ideas over all else in human experience. We conclude that what is not pure idea is obviously tainted; therefore, we seek a life of the mind that is free of contact with the material. But the spiritual is always known in relationship to the material, which is what other- ness tells us. What we perceive is always more than it seems. It points beyond itself. It is an other that reflects both our own seeing and the inexhaustibility of what is perceived. The image, the icon or the idol, has by its very nature the capacity of transparency—enabling us to see beyond it while knowing that it somehow partakes of the other- ness to which it points. In the preface to a collection of stories about the Korean Zen Master Seung Sahn, Stephen Mitchell writes:

> Somebody comes into the Zen Center with a lighted cigarette, walks up to the Buddha-statue, blows smoke in its face and drops ashes in its lap. . . . This person has understood that nothing is holy or unholy. *All things in the universe are one, and that one is himself.* So everything is permitted. Ashes are Buddha; Buddha is ashes. The cigarette flicks. The ashes drop. But his understanding is only partial. He has not yet understood that all things are just as they are. Holy is holy; unholy is unholy. Ashes are ashes; Buddha is Buddha.[20]

The Buddha is an idol; the Buddha is not an idol. The idol is not nec- essary; the idol is necessary.

If we make too much of the encounter with the wholly other, we are likely to find our ease with some idol that prevents us from continued growth in relation to the wholly other. But that does not mean that we can do without the idol, which is the memory of the encounter. When it is ignored, there will be others that take its place. They, too, will tend to be unrecognized, but nevertheless effective.

In *Moby Dick* Ishmael compares whaling with the destructiveness of warfare. There are those who consider whalers and soldiers to be butchers alike. But, says Ishmael, the sperm whaleship is among "the cleanliest things of this tidy earth," not at all like the defilement of battlefields.

---

[20]Stephen Mitchell, ed., *Dropping Ashes on the Buddha* (New York: Grove Press, 1976) ix.

What disordered slippery decks of a whale-ship are comparable to the unspeakable carrion of those battle-fields from which so many soldiers return to drink in all ladies' plaudits? And if the idea of peril so much enhances the popular conceit of the soldier's profession; let me assure ye that many a veteran who has fully marched up to a battery, would quickly recoil at the apparition of the sperm whale's vast tail, fanning into eddies the air over his head. For what are the comprehensible terrors of man compared with the interlinked terrors and wonders of God![21]

Those "interlinked terrors and wonders" portray the singular, representative, and wholly other nature of existence.

---

[21]Herman Melville, *Moby Dick* (New York: Modern Library, 1950) 107.

V / The Contemplation of Otherness

Recently it was said by a great scientific historian that the day of the literary naturalist is done, that the precision of the laboratory is more and more encroaching upon that individual domain. I am convinced that this is a mistaken judgment. We forget—as Bacon did not forget—that there is a natural history of souls, nay, even of himself, that can be learned only from the symbolism inherent in the world *about him.*

It is the natural history that led Hudson to glimpse eternity in some old men's faces at Land's End, that led Thoreau to see human civilizations as toadstools sprung up in the night by solitary roads, or that provoked Melville to experience in the sight of a sperm whale some colossal alien existence without which man himself would be incomplete.

"There is no Excellent Beauty that hath not some strangeness in the Proportion," wrote Bacon in his days of insight. Anyone who has picked up shells on a strange beach can confirm his observation. But modern man, who has not contemplated his otherness, *the multiplicity of other possible people who dwell or might have dwelt in him, has not realized the full terror and responsibility of existence.*[1]

$\mathbf{F}$or Loren Eiseley, there was a "symbolism inherent in the world," a *more than* in the midst of all our seeing and hearing, our

---

[1] Loren Eiseley, *The Night Country* (New York: Charles Scribner's Sons, 1971) 148.

analysis and evaluation. To be aware of this prepares one for a more honest and responsible understanding of self and world. It seems to be a gift of sight and insight, the kind that creates an Einstein or, in Eiseley's terms, a Hudson, a Thoreau, or a Melville, who encounters the mystery and meaning of otherness in a sperm whale. The contemplation of otherness becomes the most essential human task. Is it too much to say that it is basic to scholarship and education, to the artistic and scientific enterprises?

The problem with contemplation is that it sounds like some fanciful venture into absurdity. It seems a rather soft-headed business, quite distinct from the agenda of the analytical scholar. Yet, if my description of existence as the encounters of otherness is valid, then the search for knowledge and understanding must entertain principles that are appropriate to the facts of the situation—and that is hard-headed thinking, not harmless musing and speculation. The intellectual enterprise has become, on the one hand, an affair of extremely academic gamesmanship, and on the other, an exercise of technical reason designed to solve problems. We have not, as Eiseley says, contemplated our otherness. We have lost appreciation for the fact of otherness, and contemplation is no longer in the range of our experience. Yet contemplation is the intellectual quality most appropriate to the search for knowledge and understanding. Contemplation is the umbrella under which all other intellectual and rational activities must be done, because it is the activity appropriate to the dynamic character of existence as the encounters with otherness.

Contemplation is the first principle in the development of a grammar of religious studies. Ishmael contemplated the nature of his strange voyage aboard the *Pequod*:

> Now that I recall all the circumstances, I think I can see a little into the springs and motives, which being cunningly presented to me under various disguises, induced me to set about performing the part I did, besides cajoling me into the delusion that it was a choice resulting from my own unbiased freewill and discriminating judgement.

He has acquired the perspective for understanding the motives behind his adventure and the nature of the voyage itself. He brings little preconception and considerable openness to the process of understanding. He attacks nothing; rather, he is somehow aware of his own close but mysterious relationship to the world around him. He learns by giving himself in wonder.

> Chief among these motives was the overwhelming idea of the great whale himself. Such a portentous and mysterious monster aroused my curiosity. Then the wild and distant seas where he rolled his island bulk; the undeliverable nameless perils of the whale; these with all the attending marvels of a thousand Patagonian sights and sounds, helped to sway me to my wish.[2]

Ishmael speaks without extravagances, yet with an extraordinary awareness of the singular, representative, and wholly otherness of existence. How different from Ahab's obsession! Ishmael's reflection suggests a grammar appropriate to the study of all things, especially religion. And what is most important, the grammar begins with contemplation.

A grammar includes the rules of language. It is the science of things said and written. Grammar makes clarification, communication, and understanding possible. Grammar is the principle of correlation between what is said and what is understood. To consider a grammar of religious studies is to reflect upon those principles that are essential to understanding the evidences of religion as the encounters with otherness. When we think about what it is we are doing as religion scholars, we stand with Ishmael. He recognizes the fact that his experience is somehow laid upon him as an assignment—he has been "induced . . . to see about performing the part [he] did. . . ." Chief among the factors in his inducement was the realization that what was before him was overwhelming and mysterious. It was not something to be subdued or manipulated, yet it yielded to observation and investigation. It was a response to the *more than* that was evident in the midst of ordinarily observable reality. Ishmael responds by way of contemplation to the evidence of dynamic otherness. Contemplation will bring understanding. It is the key principle in his grammar of voyaging, and suggests to us an example for our own voyaging as scholars of religion.

Contemplation is not out of harmony with the fundamental expectation behind and beneath all study. We study in order to develop critical skills—habits and techniques of judgment. It is probably fair to say

---

[2]Herman Melville, *Moby Dick* (New York: Modern Library, 1950) 6.

that we seek to do criticism, strive for aptitude in it. Yet the reason for criticism is remarkably simple and direct. Criticism enables us to get to the heart of the matter. We are really asking, How did something really happen? How does something really work? What does something really say? How does something really look? The aim of all true criticism is much akin to the German historian Leopold von Ranke's definition of the purpose of history: finding out "wie es wirklich gewesen ist" ("how it really was").

It is my contention that the purposes of contemplation and criticism are one and the same and that the methods of both need not be antagonistic. Dostoyevsky, in *The Brothers Karamazov*, makes this observation:

> There is a remarkable picture called Contemplation. It shows a forest in winter and on a roadway through the forest, in absolute solitude, stands a peasant in torn kaftan, and bark shoes. He stands, as it were, lost in thought. Yet he is not thinking: he is "contemplating." If anyone touched him he would start and look bewildered. In time he would come to himself immediately; but if he were asked what he had been thinking about, he would remember nothing. Yet probably he has hidden within himself, the impression which dominated him during the period of contemplation. Those impressions are dear to him and he probably hoards them imperceptibly, and even unconsciously. How and why, of course, he does not know. He may suddenly, after hoarding impressions for many years, abandon everything and go off to Jerusalem on a pilgrimage. Or he may suddenly set fire to his native village. Or he may do both.[3]

Dostoyevsky seems to describe a mental process that penetrates beneath the usual processes of active and technical reason. It collects impressions with which the self identifies. One might describe this process as elemental thought. Presumably we learn to discriminate among these contemplative impressions; however, it is always possible for us to utilize these impressions according to our selective wills.

In the history of religions we discover that contemplation has a more disciplined history. Here contemplation means training in a mental process that is superordinary, or at least *extra*ordinary. Con-

---

[3]Fyodor Dostoyevsky, *The Brothers Karamazov* (New York: American Library, 1957) 123.

templation takes the random "not thinking" of Dostoyevsky's peasant and trains it so that the results will be both personally and ethically beneficial. While the results cannot be manipulated, they can be made more probable than usual. When we read the writings of those whose lives have been devoted to contemplation, we discover minds that are extraordinarily insightful, minds in which intelligence is united to will for the benefit of self and the world. These people seem to see and understand on a level quite different from many of us—at least most of the time. They have learned to expand the horizons of the elemental thought of Dostoyevsky's peasant. In fact, they have learned that this transformed mind commits their wills to thoughts and actions that are for the good of the neighbor. They would not "set fire to [their] native village[s]" unless such action were the only benevolent solution—perhaps to rid the people of a communicable disease.

What we discover in contemplation is what we expect of the art of criticism. We wish to see deeply, to understand things as they really are. The Anglican theologian, Austin Farrer, discussing the nature of poetic truth, remarked:

> I count poetical vision and even amatory passion the friends of religion, in spite of the fact that their abuse may easily tend the other way. But though poetry often breeds an attitude of fancifulness and egotism; and love, heaven knows, of animality and complacency; yet we have on the other side to set this—that *the lover and the poet at least look at something and see it*. And the chief impediment to religion in this age, I often think, is that no one ever looks at anything at all: not so as *to contemplate* it, to apprehend what it is to be that thing, and plumb, if he can, the deep fact of its individual existence. The mind rises from the knowledge of creatures to the knowledge of their creator, but this does not happen through the sort of knowledge which can analyze things into factors or manipulate them with technical skill or classify them into groups.[4]

I would only add to Farrer's insight by suggesting that the sort of knowledge that analyzes, manipulates, and classifies may itself be transformed so that contemplation takes place and knowledge becomes, in a sense, transcendent. To the extent that the scientist discovers things *as they really are* in the midst of his analysis,

---

[4]Austin Farrer, *Reflective Faith* (Grand Rapids: Eerdmans, 1974) 37-38.

manipulation, and classification, he has already recognized the *more than* in the midst of things. Of course, there are also scholars devoted to this sort of knowledge whose lives and writings attest to their discovery of how it really is. The principle is not new by any means; it has been basic to many of the world's religions. Judaism, in both its rabbinic and kabbalistic forms, attests to this. Jacob Neusner points out the relentless criticism that was practiced by rabbis who commented on the Mishnah. Behind all their activity was

> the remarkable claim that in the give and take of argument, in the processes of criticism, you do something transcendent, more than this-worldly. I cannot overemphasize how remarkable is the combination of rational criticism and the supernatural value attached to it. You simply cannot understand Rabbinic Judaism without confronting this other-worldly context.[5]

This notion of the supernatural need not frighten away those who are theistically indifferent. What is being said is that the actions of criticism are accompanied by a commitment to the truth. The key to what is meaningful and real is discovered by criticism. One assumption of any critical activity is that we do not see and understand things as they really are except by some such mental process.

I return now to the discussion of contemplation. The term is often associated with a style of spiritual life that is monastic and devoted to the rigors of personal transformation. Discussions of spiritual progress in the West tend to agree on three stages: purification, illumination, and union with God. The literature attendant to this process may sometimes tend to be heavily tropaic and even erotic. It may also change the terminology used to designate the three stages. The unprepared reader is likely to be frightened by the extravagance. He may prejudge the material as pathological, naive, or elitist. He senses that he is in very alien territory. Were he to overcome his religious awkwardness or biases, he would discover principles that are in harmony with the purposes of criticism.

"Contemplation," said St. John of the Cross, "is the mystical theology which theologians call secret wisdom which St. Thomas says is

---

[5]Jacob Neusner, *Between Time and Eternity. The Essentials of Judaism* (Belmont: Wadsworth Publishing Company, 1975) 68-69.

communicated and infused into the soul through love." This is an example of the kind of language that might be stereotyped by scholars without much consideration for its theory of knowledge. Perhaps a paraphrase will restore its credibility: contemplation is that caring way of looking at the world which makes one aware of the truth that is generally hidden beneath the surface of ordinary knowledge. To be certain, the contemplative usually encounters a reality that he feels is beyond the scope of linguistic description. "The ascetic," writes Archimandrite Sophrony, "in spiritual contemplation beholds things which for the overwhelming majority of people are a mystery, but afterwards he is faced with the impossibility of communicating this mystery—translated into mortal language it is construed quite differently by him who hears it."[6]

Actually, in this there may be a misunderstanding, rather a misapprehension. Perhaps the spiritual contemplative misses the same element in his activity as does the skeptical critic. A person's language is very limited in its capacity to convey an inner state to someone else. As Sophrony himself puts it, "The indispensible condition for mutual understanding is a common or identical experience."[7] Yet how is it possible to be aware of a common or identical experience unless some form of communication takes place?

What one encounters in contemplation is not any more difficult to communicate by language, symbol, or ritual than any other form of profound human experience. This is so because any encounter is with otherness in its singular and representative forms, and with its wholeness. The spiritual contemplative assumes one cannot speak because one has encountered an *absolute* other; however, as noted, this wholly other is a wholeness in which that person lives, moves, and has being. Accordingly, the mystery of which Sophrony speaks is always in our midst. To that extent, we can and should talk about it. If criticism is honest and thorough, it will discover that contemplation is the most comprehensive mode of inquiry. Criticism has to be more than conjecture or simple analysis (whatever that may be). It has to be more than some form of bracketing or methodological jousting. It cannot

---

[6]Archimandrite Sophrony, *The Monk of Mount Athos* (Crestwood: St. Vladimir's Seminary Press, 1973) 115.

[7]Ibid.

honestly limit itself to a process that rules out personal avowals, that ignores the dynamic encounter with otherness in all its active process. It cannot be satisfied with applying the so-called "methods" of this or that anthropologist, sociologist, or philosopher. Criticism for the religion scholar must become personally responsible and comprehensive at some point. Understandably, all of these limited and limiting devices just mentioned may be necessary at some stage in the process of critical inquiry. But true criticism will be contemplative; it will develop skills appropriate to seeing things as they really are. It will learn how to discipline the elemental impressions of Dostoyevsky's contemplative peasant.

The most valuable source for learning is the literature of contemplation itself. Whatever else such literature demonstrates, it certainly attests to the fact that human beings have had long and continuing experience with what really is. Their insights and methods are invaluable to the scholar who wants to make the same discovery. Assuredly, there are many scholars who are satisfied with discovering what they already know. They seek only to add more trivia to the conventions of some established order. But one who is honest about making discoveries cannot ignore the findings of contemplative religious thought.

Contemplation is pragmatic. The skilled contemplative knows that there have been times when he has stood like Dostoyevsky's peasant, only realizing after the fact that raw and pure impressions had overtaken him. Or there may have been times when his mind has seemed especially open, attentive in such a way that he seemed to be on the edge of unique insight and understanding. In both cases, though, the moments have passed quickly and ordinariness returned. Many of our human frustrations result from this experience. We settle for what we know is conventional, second-rate. Sometimes we live in depression or sordidness because those momentary glimpses of possibility have made us aware of our inadequacy. However, the contemplative learns that those glimpses can be understood and nurtured. The contemplative is open to the possibilities of such moments, while knowing such moments cannot be manipulated. The result of such work is usually the discovery that it is only under these conditions that things are seen as they really are. Usually one sees only what one wants to see and what one has been taught to see by the values of one's worldview.

The pragmatics is this: since it is evident that there are occasional impressions and insights that appear to get at the heart of the matter in a way that seems superior to, or at least complementary to, my ordinary thought; since, further, it becomes increasingly evident that there have been people who have devoted much of their living to the cultivation and understanding of those occasional impressions and insights; it becomes further evident that I, as a scholar, should apply such operations of the intellect to the business of critical inquiry—especially since the purpose of the latter enterprise is understanding matters as they really are. In Theravada Buddhism, the monk treads carefully the path of mindfulness. He seeks to contemplate in a most comprehensive manner every act and function of his body. As his bare foot moves along the garden trail, each part of it participates in the act of walking. The heel, the pad of the sole, the toes—each part conscious of its touchings and intentions. By this means, along with other contemplative arts, the mind moves beyond the trivia of existence, and the senses deliver active data to it. The process is similar to the "watchfulness" of Christian tradition. Kallistos Ware defines watchfulness as attentiveness, vigilance, recollection. It means "to be present *where we are*—at this specific point in space, at this particular moment of time." When we are gathered into the here and now, we see things *as they really are*, rather than according to the dictates of desire, illusion, indifference, or methodology. The intellectual and academic enterprises have paid scant attention to the workings of the mind and will as they are described by the contemplative masters of the world.

What is pragmatic is defined according to the task before us. If criticism is to help us understand things as they really are, it stands to gain much from a contemplative approach to its task. What is being said here is similar to what Austin Farrer says of the importance of theology. It is not a luxury, wrote Farrer. One's faith must be lived as well as thought, but without thought it can't be lived. There is really no difference between "plain practical religion" and "theology." A faith that is undefined and unexpressed is hardly practical.[8] One may well ask whether it is practical to attempt to learn the significance of something only by manipulating and limiting it, never asking, "what *is*

---

[8]Charles C. Hefling, Jr., *Jacob's Ladder* (Cambridge: Cowley Publications, 1979) 40.

this?" There are two assumptions that should be rejected in this regard. First, to ask "what *is* this" is not to rely upon intuition. Recent discussions by advocates of various forms of esoteric religion such as hesychasm, Sufism, and Zen Buddhism tend to speak of the recovery of the intuitive mind. I believe this to be a mistake. The question of the use of reason and the intellect is a matter of context. For those interested in contemplation, the question before them is, How can the context of the mind be opened, expanded, to the point where it is receptive to experience and truth not ordinarily available? In its expansive context, the mind will contrive to be critical and evaluative. However, it will be a criticism much less manipulative, suppressive, and inhibiting than is usually the case.

A second assumption to be guarded against is the notion that describing life as it really is represents a narrow dogmatism. If we find ourselves saying to someone, "No! *This* is the way it really is! This is the correct understanding!," we have already demonstrated that we are not being critical enough. A truly contemplative approach to understanding is ever aware of the snare positivism poses to the mind. To see what really is is to encounter the dramatic character of otherness in its singular, representative, and wholly forms. Recall, too, that the most perceptive and unfettered of such encounters always contains an element of mystery that qualifies our seeing what really is.

Zen Buddhism illustrates the point I am making. Perhaps the most elusive of all intellectual traditions, its evasions are not nearly so absolute as its interpreters often suggest. For example, Thomas Hoover: "Zen became the religion of the antirational, what might be called the counter mind." It aligns itself with "our intuitive, nonverbal perception and understanding." Then Hoover goes on to say that "Zen masters have *deliberately* developed techniques (like illogical riddles or koan) to discredit the logical, verbal side of the mind so that the intuitive perceptions of the right hemisphere, the counter mind, may define reality."[9] How, then, is reality defined by the mind? If it is defined at all, we may be certain that critical skills are at work. Hoover devotes his book to the influence of Zen on Chinese and Japanese culture. He writes of the "arts of the counter mind" and invites us to see "what the

---

[9]Thomas Hoover, *Zen Culture* (New York: Random House, 1978) 4-5.

intuitive side of the mind can *produce*." It is not likely that it is counter mind or intuition that produces a culture of distinctive art, military styles, aesthetics, and psychology. I suggest that the critical skills undergo transformation in the expanding context of a mind that gives itself to the encounter of things as they really are. The result is that the critical skills are used in a new way, perhaps a more creative and integral way.

How is contemplation to be used as a means of critical inquiry? The first of the three stages of contemplation is purification, which also offers an important first step for the critical inquiry into otherness. The uninitiated reader will probably assume that purification refers to some kind of private purge of immorality. Taking his cue from American evangelical notions of morality as involving abstinence from food, drink, and sexual relations, the uninitiated may very well recoil in scholarly and academic horror from any suggestion that purification could have anything to do with the art and science of criticism. Somehow there is a connotation of inhibition associated with purification that seems inimical to criticism.

A closer look at the contemplative heritage may allay these fears. In discussing prayer as an element of contemplation, Kallistos Ware writes:

> We are not to restrict God's presence in the world to a limited range of "pious" objects and situations, while labelling everything else as "secular"; but we are to see all things as essentially sacred, as a gift from God and a means of communion with him. It does not, however, follow that we are to accept the fallen world on its own terms. This is the mistake of much "secular Christianity" in the contemporary west. All things are indeed sacred in their true being, according to their innermost essence; but our relationship to God's creation has been distorted by sin . . . and we shall not rediscover this intrinsic sacredness unless our heart is purified. Without self-denial, without ascetic discipline, we cannot affirm the true beauty of the world. That is why there can be no genuine contemplation without repentance.[10]

What is notable in the above quote is the reality of the encounter with otherness. Paraphrasing, we cannot restrict the range of other-

---

[10]Kallistos Ware, *The Orthodox Way* (Crestwood: St. Vladimir's Seminary Press, 1979) 160-61.

ness in the world to a listing of "objects and situations." The otherness is comprehensive—it is wholly other, even in its representative and singular manifestations. However, we are accustomed to making restrictions in the light of our assumptions, private desires, and limited purposes. Unless the heart is purified, contemplation of otherness is not possible. Accordingly, there are two elements that become fundamental to the process of purification. They are repentance and ascetic discipline.

Repentance is another term charged with the trappings of personal piety. It may be repulsive to some of the overly self-righteous. Despite this, it is a good word, and an essential component in reaching the goals of critical inquiry. We wish to be purified, which means that we must rid our intellect and reason of the clutter that prevents us from seeing what really is. We wish to minimize the effect of the lenses through which our seeing is done. Some contemplatives would maintain that it is possible to remove the lenses entirely. Whether this is possible or not, it should be the goal, at some crucial stage of our scholarly work, to do more than test a theory or a method. That which we encounter should not be seen and known only as a representative other. The person is more than male or female, father or mother, taxpayer, consumer, reformer, philosopher, or criminal. Most scholarly activity tends to be satisfied with examining the representative character of otherness. But otherness resists such classifications, making observations partial, distorted, and valid only for the second in which the object is contemplated. The singularity and wholeness of what we encounter requires a more expansive mode of inquiry.

As a result, purification becomes an essential element in the style of our work, and purification requires repentance. Repentance is always the point from which any journey is begun. The Greek word for repentance is *metanoia*, which signifies "change of mind." In the evangelical Christian tradition, repentance tends to mean primarily a conversion of the will, accompanied by the kind of emotional unrest that would likely follow such an experience. However, *metanoia* suggests a transformation of intellect as well as will. We are to change our minds. Obviously, that process is certain to be gradual. However, it is possible to recognize the error or limitation of our present perspective and turn in the direction of a more expansive and comprehensive one. We would be seeking purification; and we would begin by repenting, changing our minds in order to begin a new and different journey, an Abrahamic pilgrimage into an unknown land.

The trick in this process is to maintain the energy of our initial conversion. There is a sense in which repentance must be a continuing state. It must be renewed and maintained throughout the critical enterprise. It is ascetic discipline that is charged with supporting the nurture of repentance. "Without self-denial, without ascetic discipline, we cannot affirm the true beauty of the world." Without certain techniques and intellectual habits that direct the mind to its essential task of seeing things as they really are, we fall easy prey to attractions along the way. This is in keeping with rabbinic Judaism's "way of living *as if* and *until*—until the Messiah will come. The nonhistorical, nontimebound quality of the rabbinic mode of life and thought is for the present."[11] Hence the techniques of study, discussion, and living form a discipline that pragmatically ("as if") keeps the mind repentant and purified—free of the distractions that distort the world from day to day. The rabbis had a discipline for keeping the mind expanded to see things as they really are to a critical mind. Humanistic scholars today tend to be very conventional practitioners, writing volumes based upon some minor point in which they hope to interest at least ten other scholars. We seem less concerned with the truth, more fascinated by terminology and methodologies. Ascetic discipline is essential to the task of critical inquiry because it prevents us from facile devotion to the obsessions of the ordinary mind.

Ascesis is simply the Greek word for exercise. To many of us it has come to mean "self-torture," but we must sidestep our rather immature judgments about the monks and anchorites of the earliest days of Christianity. Whether or not there have been excesses associated with asceticism, the fact remains that such matters must be studied in the context of their theology, time, and circumstances. Here it is sufficient to point out that the ascetic way is the discipline followed to achieve a certain end. A discipline is a direction, a pointing of the way. Any discipline involves saying "no" to certain things in order to say "yes" to others. Ascetic discipline is necessary to the process of purification that will enable us to reach, by critical inquiry, the greatest possible truth. The self-indulgent individual usually acquires little understand-

---

[11]Neusner, *Between Time and Eternity*, 111.

ing of things as they really are because his ideas, imagination, and feelings are attached to a fleeting and restricted selfhood. The best scholar is always saying "no" to whims and fancies, to partial claims, because he understands that the center of truth is somewhere "out there."

The insightful scholar finds the means of turning away from his current desires because he realizes that what he has already learned and understood is but a foretaste—the presence of the *more than* in the midst. In turning away from the world (which is the limitation of reality to present desire and understanding), he experiences a change in his relationship to truth. The truth is no longer something to be possessed; it is there to be encountered, and becomes present and personal. The sense of center is no longer inside the self, but in the encounter with truth. Just as repentance is a step in the direction of greater purity, so ascetic discipline establishes purity as a condition most conducive to the quest for understanding what really is. Purification by any other name is an essential stage in the pursuit of criticism. It is not a state of propriety and nicety, not a condition of sanctimonious innocence. Purification is a state of honesty, in which the mind has been relieved of prized assumptions and expectations that impede the expansive quest.

The problem with much contemporary scientific inquiry is that it is not aware of its own soul: it cannot gauge what it knows and does not know. Presumably, what has happened is that the intellectual and scholarly guilds have become disenchanted with the authoritarian nature of previous human history. However, they have wrongly assumed that authoritarianism belongs to the past, that they themselves are free of its darkness. They have been strongly inclined to identify authoritarianism with religion, while often substituting for it an authoritarian science or criticism. Such attitudes are not easy to exorcise. We must learn to recognize them, repent, and develop the discipline that assists us in purifying our minds and preparing them for transformation.

There are scientists and critics who know this. For them, contemplation has already become the proper mode of inquiry. They already recognize that the inquiry must begin with openness, with doubt, with a reverent attention to the *more than* in the midst of things. Loren Eiseley comments:

Physicists are convinced that a principle of uncertainty exists in the sub-microscopic realm of particles and that out of this queer domain of accident and impact has emerged, by some kind of mathematical magic, the sustaining world of natural law by which we make our way to the bank, theatre, to our homes, and finally to our graves. Perhaps, after all, a world so created has something still wild and unpredictable lurking behind its more sober manifestations.[12]

If there is that rare freedom of a particle to do what is unexpected, it means that our existence consists of the constant encounter with an otherness that is more than our measure of it. To know such a "wild and unpredictable" possibility requires the posture of contemplation, disciplined into a purified stance of uncertainty.

How much more we would see, I sometimes think, if the world were lit solely by lightning flashes from the Elizabethan stage. What miraculous insights and perceptions might our senses be trained to receive amidst the alternate crash of thunder and the hurtling force that give a peculiar and momentary shine to an old tree on a wet night. Our world might be transformed interiorly from its staid arrangement of laws and uniformity of expression into one where the unexpected and blinding illumination constituted our faith in reality.[13]

That, of course, is the second stage in the contemplative process. Where purification is in process, there is the possibility of "the unexpected and blinding illumination." However fleeting and spasmodic the illumination may be, it begins to be the criterion of what truth is— it constitutes "our faith in reality." It is fragile, not to be possessed or harnessed to our specifications.

It would be difficult for anyone to deny that what they seek is illumination. Certainly a glimpse of light where darkness abides is the most genuine and ardent of our desires as scholars. Light is associated with truth, and each of us knows that truth is elusive. Because it seems evasive, we are often impatient, creating in advance our own images of what the illumination should be. Illumination that is the object of our definition and formation is not illumination at all. It is a creature of our darkness. The ordinary mind makes distinctions be-

---

[12]Eiseley, *The Night Country*, 136.

[13]Ibid.

tween light and dark that are, at best, derived from a residue of wisdom, from a filament of memory of past illumination. Light is the unexpected revelation that comes to the seeker who is constantly at work purifying his mind through repentance and ascetic discipline. Demonstrating these qualities is not the closet activity of the eccentric or precocious mind. They must become the work of the disciplined scholar in the course of his occupation.

Matter, as discussed, is no longer solidity and bulk, but waves of energy. Energy is the movement of light radiating through the universe, the constant reflection of the primeval fireball. Perhaps this light is the process of consciousness itself. When we speak of illumination, the scientist and the humanist confront the same reality. In the previous century, James Clark Maxwell provided a harmony to the theories of light, electricity, and magnetism. To that integration of theory was added the work of numerous scientists and theorists who left us with the possibility of envisioning reality in a way that contradicts the ordinary mind. We need only develop attitudes and disciplines that prepare us for the encounter with what really is: the realm of illumination of which we are part.

Even though seeing things as they really are is not the work of the ordinary mind, it is nevertheless the work of the mind. When the critic is visited with insight into one of his investigations, he is able to recognize the insight. This means that the mind already possesses a predisposition for the light, but makes foreclosures against the very illumination it seeks. Contemplation, as a mode of inquiry, does its best to pull the mind toward its original disposition. All knowledge is knowledge of otherness; but, as we have seen, otherness always includes us and is eternal process, eternal consciousness. The only perception is perception of an other. As an other, the perceived is known only in relationship to me.

Otherness is always more than any perception. Consequently, illumination will always be momentary. Even though it may be akin to what the mystic calls ineffable, inexplicable, its light will always shine on something, someone. Neither the light nor what it illumines can ever be complete, final, or absolute; there is always more. What we call matter and spirit are constantly involved and interrelated. Matter may be energy, light, consciousness, to the theories of pure science. However, there is no pure science, only scientists who achieve sufficient purification to experience illumination. Ordinarily, the mind must function according to the demands of an existence that forecloses against illumination. The wise person will be the one who patiently permits illumination to increase his loyalty and trust in the wholly other, of which we are given occasional glimpses as we critically seek to know it.

The scholar and the immature religionist often have something in common: impatience. One of America's early teachers of Zen Buddhism spoke of these people: "Without waiting for the fruit to ripen, they open up their stores and begin to sell their wares. Such unripened fruit is unhealthy, and may cause injury to those who do not know the difference."[14] Patience and maturity are themselves the virtues of those who have learned the art of contemplation. Instead of the desire to possess, they have found a way to be open, to relate. Instead of the desire to dissect, they have learned to embrace. Instead of the desire to bracket, they have discovered the way of fence razing. Possession, dissection, and bracketing are signals of impatience and foreclosure. They are only useful after contemplation has shown us what really is. Even then their value is temporary, allowing us to clarify and interpret with the ordinary mind what has been revealed to us.

Purification and illumination will lead us to dynamic union with the wholly other, the *more than* in our midst. So say the contemplative writers, those whom we often call mystics. However, if we examine what that means in the language of the critic, the words may not seem so mysterious. Why is it that, as critics, we wish to learn what really is? No genuine scholar can be satisfied with learning less. We may assume that we discover what really is by all of our conventional attempts to possess, dissect, or bracket. We make that assumption because it is necessary to our well-being to know that we are dealing with truth, not falsehood. If someone told us we were dealing with less than the truth, it would bother us—even if we were philosophical enough to believe that truth is relative and dynamic.

To discern the truth, to know what really is, is important to us for religious and ethical reasons. Religiously, we need to feel that we have a view of reality that sustains us; ethically, we want to value what is

---

[14]Louis Nordstrom, ed., *Namu Dai Bosa. A Transmission of Zen Buddhism to America* (New York: Theatre Arts Books, 1976) 48.

good and live our lives accordingly. The same impulses are common to scholars. The critical task has both religious and ethical dimensions. As critics, we wish to be united with what really is. A sense of being at one with the truth is basic to our role as scholars. However occasional it may be, the illumination we receive provides us with a foretaste of what union with the truth is really like.

The effect of illumination often makes us aware of the darkness in which we reside. Like Socrates and Plato, we begin to realize how little we understand. We discover that it is our task to pursue the mystery of truth. Our illumination helps us to realize that the unknown is in the midst of every known. What we encounter is the wholly other, that which is comparably greater than what we say or know about it. It is like the knowledge of a loved one; rather than possessing or defining absolutely, we encounter an other whom we know by being one with her or him. All that we affirm by our statements about the other is less than the truth because otherness is a mystery.

The best way of talking about truth is by means of what Eastern Orthodoxy calls the "apophatic" approach. We must learn to use negative statements, sometimes saying what reality is *not* rather than what it is. This is because the wholly other that we encounter is personal. It could not be otherwise, for all observation participates in what it observes; matter is basically energy, consciousness; and the very fact of otherness means that we create and are created by the others we encounter. Vladimir Lossky argues that:

> Excluding concepts, personhood cannot be defined. It is the incomparable, the wholly-other. One can only add up individuals, not persons. The person is always unique. The concept objectifies and collects. Only a thought methodically "deconceptualized" by apophasis can evoke the mystery of personhood. For that which remains irreducible to every nature cannot be defined, but only designated.[15]

The proper relationship to the truth is union, oneness, as with a person. The appropriate manner of intellectualization is apophasis— a kind of iconoclasm. Apophatic thinking knows that all we affirm concerning truth, however correct, falls far short of the *living* truth. Re-

---

[15]Vladimir Lossky, *Orthodox Theology: An Introduction* (Crestwood: St. Vladimir's Seminary Press, 1978) 42-43.

pentance and ascetic discipline, used in our work as critics, will help to guarantee the negative style of apophasis, and assure the continuing process of purification, illumination, and union in the pursuit of truth. As Kallistos Ware states it: "The apophatic way of 'unknowing' brings us not to emptiness but to fullness. Our negations are in reality super-affirmations. Distractive in outward form, the apophatic approach is affirmative in its final effects: it helps us to reach out, beyond all statements positive or negative"[16] toward encounter with the truth. Giles Gunn refers to an essay by Benjamin DeMott in which the latter claimed that

> Americans today suffer from a distinctive, though by no means exclusively American, form of myopia. Our national commitment to the ideal of personal self-fulfillment, together with our equally strong counterdesire to achieve an ego-transcending oneness of identity with other people, are two sides of the same coin. . . . Both represent a rejection of the idea that the realization of humanness, whether for oneself alone or for an entire group, "depends," as he put it, "upon my capacity and my desire to make real to myself the inward life, the subjective reality of the lives that are lived beyond me."[17]

This subjective reality is the otherness we encounter in all beings partly because we ourselves are doing the observing. It is at the heart of the quest for truth; it is personal, and the art of contemplation is the proper mode of inquiry.

---

[16]Ware, *The Orthodox Way*, 17.

[17]Giles Gunn, *The Interpretation of Otherness* (New York: Oxford University Press, 1979) 175-76.

VI / Contemplation
and the Art of
Reading and Study

When Zarathustra had spoken these words he beheld the people again and was silent. "There they stand," he said to his heart, "there they laugh. They do not understand me; I am not the mouth for these ears. Must one smash their ears before they learn to listen with their eyes? Must one clatter like kettledrums and preachers of repentance? Or do they believe only the stammerer?

"They have something of which they are proud. What do they call that which makes them proud? Education they call it; it distinguishes them from goatherds."[1]

Like Zarathustra, many scholars speak on behalf of some curious *overman*, despising those who do not comprehend their words: "I am not the mouth for these ears." The scholar may be right to look with disdain (at least chagrin) on those who take pride in something they call education, but which merely "distinguishes them from goatherds" and adjusts their lives to mediocrity. I should like to suggest, however, that Zarathustra's discovery has another edge to it, perhaps one that Nietzsche had not intended. It is good to learn that one is not the ultimate apostle. Not all ideas are applicable to every situation. My thoughts, however profound, are not really for all ears—no matter the reason. By the same token, the words of a genius, an au-

---

[1]Walter Kaufmann, ed., *The Portable Nietzsche* (New York: Viking Press, 1961) 128.

thority, are expendable. I may not need them for the task I am doing, even though their absence seems unforgivable in the minds of the "educated" guild who distinguish themselves from goatherds. "I am not the mouth for these ears" is a bit of wisdom that may apply to the words I write. It is likely to be important for all scholars to remember.

The style of contemplation that confronts us with what really is illuminates and unites us to the truth, not to our *comprehension* of it. The truth is always wholly other. The words I use to describe it may be sufficient for me; and they may be adequate for a section meeting of the American Academy of Religion, or even the American Philosophical Society. However, they are not the truth itself. And it is always possible for me to discover that "I am not the mouth for these ears." Nor may Turner, Lonergan, Gadamer, Geertz, or Watras be the mouths for *my* ears. What all this adds up to is a plea for catholicity and humility among scholars. In this way, the conventions will open up a bit, be more responsive to the serious and common task of bringing understanding to ourselves and others. The elitism of an establishment is already with us and threatens to destroy our enterprise.[2] Much of it is supported, of course, by systems of tenure and promotion in an academic climate where employment is scarce. In circumstances such as these, conformity in scholarship becomes a dangerous reality. One observes it in the "refereeing" practices of journals, the selection of lecturers, and the hiring of faculty in colleges and universities. It is time to learn what Zarathustra learned: "I am not the mouth for these ears."

We who contemplate what really is should become critics. However, we are not likely to be interested in that approach unless we have learned the need for contemplation. We would have made that discovery if we had been confronted with the precarious nature of our best efforts—as indeed had Zarathustra. Only then would we be likely to enter the stage of purification and understand the value of contemplation as a mode of critical inquiry.

Attitude is important as we turn to the substance of the profession of religious studies. We work with "evidence," contemplating books, manuscripts, and other literary materials. We consider what people have said, written, thought, and done. It is our business to read and to

---

[2]Richard E. Wentz, "Is There a New Establishment of Religion?" *The Christian Century* 84:15 (12 April 1967): 463-65.

observe and to reflect. Perhaps the dominant activity among today's scholars is reading. We read primary sources, secondary sources, commentaries, essays of interpretation, and philosophical treatises. Even if we study ritual, stories, myth, and symbols, we are likely to do so by means of ethnographic materials and other written sources that record the objects of our investigations. Few of us are field scholars. Accordingly, what we do most is read. Reading is basic to our vocation and therefore literary works are highly significant.

There has been no dearth of literary output in the second half of the twentieth century. Much of it is the product of the conventionalizing of scholarship in the midst of the democratization and proliferation of higher education. People publish because they must, not because they have literary ambitions or even abilities. Some would say that much of what is produced is not really literature but glossography. We indulge ourselves in the writing of glosses, marginal explanations of details. So much of what is written may be the result of not having learned what Zarathustra was forced to accept. Nevertheless, without more authoritative judgment about appropriate use of terms like literary and literature, I shall make the functional conclusion that what is written is in some sense literary and literature. (This leaves aside for the moment the matter of what has been termed "oral literature.")

As scholars we read and what we read is literary. T. S. Eliot, in the 1956 Gideon D. Seymour Memorial Lecture at the University of Minnesota, said of criticism:

> The critic . . . is a *literary* critic if his primary interest in writing criticism, is to help his readers to understand and to enjoy. But he must have other interests, just as much as the poet himself; for the literary critic is not merely a technical expert, who has learned the rules to be observed by the writers he criticizes: the critic must be the whole man, a man with convictions and principles, and of knowledge and experience of life.[3]

Eliot stressed the point that he did not "think of enjoyment and understanding as distinct activities—one emotional and the other intel-

---

[3]T. S. Eliot, *The Frontiers of Criticism* (Ann Arbor: University of Michigan Press, 1956) 18.

lectual." He distinguished understanding from explanation, while acknowledging a possible significant role for explanation in the process of understanding. For example, one could master the vocabulary, spelling, grammar, and syntax of Chaucer (the result of explanation) without understanding the poetry. "To understand a poem comes to the same thing as to enjoy it for the right reasons."[4]

The literature we read as scholars of religion is not written for the same reason that a poem is written. Therefore, we are not faced with the same challenge to understand and to enjoy. However, the phenomena of religion are very much akin to the poems we produce. They are the tropes of our religiousness, the tropism of otherness. They express our awareness of the interplay of the encounters of otherness. As critics of "religion," critics who write about our contemplation, we must be more than technical experts and explainers. We must be whole persons, persons "with convictions and principles, and of knowledge and experience of life." Our literary works as scholars of religion form the literature of criticism. That literature should reflect our basic purpose: to understand and to enjoy what really is. We should use this criterion in turning to those other works that claim our readership as scholars. If they do not communicate the involvement of the whole person, if they do not help us to understand and enjoy religion, they are of inferior quality and of questionable value for our continuing work.

We may recall the words of Ishmael, as he contemplated the reason for his voyage.

> Chief among these motives was the overwhelming idea of the great whale himself. Such a portentous and mysterious monster roused all my curiosity. Then the wild and distant seas where he rolled his island bulk; the undeliverable, nameless perils of the whale; thus, with all the attending marvels of a thousand Patagonian sights and sounds, helped to sway me to my wish.[5]

Fascinated by the range of otherness in all of its forms—its singularity, representativeness, and awesome wholeness—Ishmael's understand-

---

[4]Ibid., 16-17.

[5]Herman Melville, *Moby Dick* (New York: Modern Library, 1950) 6.

ing of the precarious journey is attended by a deep joy. He remains the model for our own contemplation as well.

Our humanity depends on our awareness of our otherness. We have discovered that while we are distinct beings, we are simultaneously limited by our participation in the being we contemplate. To have acquired this otherness means to have put aside the instinct that marks the animal world. As Reinhold Niebuhr was fond of saying, we became conscious of our finitude. The mind begins to know that it has lost something. We belong, yet do not belong, to everything we contemplate. We are finite, yet seem to be part of some infinite mystery. So we find ourselves trying to comprehend the "behind" and "before"—the mind seeks knowledge in order to understand as much as it can of this mystery. The mind recites what it feels and knows about the separation and the atonement of existence. The mind recites; the body dances. We sing about the strange and wonderful voyage. We work at disciplines that encourage the mind's ability to comprehend and appreciate its otherness. Our behavior and the way we plan and organize the range of our finite existence—these factors are shaped by what the mind knows. This is religion. All of this forms the field of contemplation for the scholar of religion.

However, in order to study religion, it is also necessary to study what others have collected and written about religion. Such materials are also in themselves part of religion. Anything that has participated in the contemplation of otherness is within range of our further examination. It may very well be true that I learn a great deal about religion by reading another scholar's interpretation of some subject of contemplation. I may understand and enjoy a work of critical literature and at the same time enhance my understanding and enjoyment of religion. The two experiences are inseparable if the critical work is one of integrity. Even if a critical work tends to expose the demonic underside of some cult or period in religious history, it does so by virtue of a devotion to the mystery of otherness.

Many works by scholars of religion are even more directly a part of the literature of religion. In these instances the critic understands it to be a personal obligation to speak on behalf of the mystery of otherness in a manner that virtually *recites* what has been discovered by reading other scholars. It could readily be the case in our times that my "religion" (in some conscious sense) is actually formed by my contemplation of otherness in the world of another scholar. In the 1960s, during the period of the "death-of-God" and secular theologies in Christianity and Judaism, many scholars and intellectuals found their own religiousness stimulated by the ideas and metaphors of Thomas J. J. Altizer, Richard Rubenstein, William Hamilton, and Harvey Cox. However all this may be, the scholar of religion is faced with those elements of human culture that reflect the contemplation of otherness—this includes the work of other scholars. Increasingly, the scholar is faced with what seems to be an unmanageable assignment. Contemplation, therefore, must be done according to a grammar. There are rules and principles to follow in order to manage the unwieldy task.

The first element in the grammar of contemplation is selectivity. Who can possibly read all that is available? Is it really possible to read all that is both good and relevant to one's interest? Perhaps some scholars, those who are patient through the years, are able to perform "responsibly" in this regard. They may "know all of the literature," as the saying goes. This fact does not eliminate the question of whether it is *necessary* to "know all of the literature." Much of the reason for knowing all of the literature is derived from the conventionalization of scholarship. Each of us, as contemporary scholars, has a field or a subfield. In addition, we are conscious of the fact that the larger convention of scholars has begun to use a certain vocabulary and to refer to the names of certain other scholars inside and outside the convention.

In principle, this is all to be expected and may very well enhance the understanding of religion. However, it is our purpose to contemplate so that we may understand and enjoy. We may use whatever is necessary *for us* in the pursuit of our purpose. If anything that is merely conventional interferes with our purpose, it is suspect. If it assists the scholar, it is valid. The proper criteria of judgment are always to be derived from the purpose. Conceivably I may investigate a given set of issues and succeed in the purpose of religious studies, but with little recourse to the vocabulary and names of the convention.

Frequently academic discussions become expositions of the obvious or commonplace. We have all listened to colloquia where several people turn the deliberations into a consideration of some "ism" or of "Smith's" theory. If one has not previously encountered "Smith" or the "ism," it may be difficult to follow at first. Most often one discovers that what is being discussed is a quite ordinary set of ideas or a concept that one has been using without knowing of "Smith's" work at all. It becomes increasingly evident that scholars are either lacking in imagination and common rationality, or else they are fascinated by the conventionalizations of the guild that end in sophisticated jargon and one-upmanship. It is quite possible in our day of scholarly proliferation to lose all sense of proportion and to lack a principle of selectivity in relation to what must be read. Most of what other scholars tell me I should read may be readily dismissed, because much of what is being published may be either tiring minutiae or the trivial recitation of theories.

It should be possible for most of us to arrive at certain decisions about what is to be contemplated. For instance, I can readily set some broad perimeters for the critical pursuit of a given project by defining a set of questions or issues. Naturally, these perimeters will always be expanding. The body of "research material" is always greater than the original estimate. However, I should be able to adjust the limitations of my inquiry without great difficulty. As I selectively read the appropriate materials, the schema of interpretation should begin to suggest itself to me. There may be times when I require a nudge of the imagination by someone else's language or hermeneutic. However, I am not accountable for knowing all of the languages and hermeneutical ploys, unless hermeneutics itself is the subject of my inquiry.

As a critical inquirer and interpreter, I am responsible for discovering *what is* and interpreting and reporting it adequately. I may be able to perform this task without using certain theoreticians or their terminology, without even having read their material. The point is that contemplation as critical inquiry requires selectivity. One cannot, should not, need not, read everything that the convention seems to require. Certain things may distract me, may keep me from discovering what really *is*. Therefore, I must say "no" to some things and "yes" to others. Otherwise I will also be distracted from my critical assignment by the unlimited weight of conventionally relevant material.

In critical inquiry there are two canons to be considered. First, there is the canon of sources. There is usually a long and established tradition from which I may draw in order to pursue my assignment. That tradition will define the beginnings of my contemplation as a scholar. If I wish to learn what has defined the American religious mind in the mid-nineteenth century, I must begin with a canon of sources. I may decide that it is necessary to depart from the canon, or to contemplate what have previously been peripheral sources, but the canon is there and it will affect my findings. The canon of sources influences my inquiry even if I turn from Horace Bushnell, John W. Nevin, and Ralph W. Emerson, to Walt Whitman or to the folktales of the emergent industrial era. Nevertheless, the problem of selectivity in relation to the canon of sources is a relatively easy one to manage. In critical inquiry I do not contemplate whatever gods may be or according to the precepts of revelation; I contemplate those forms of otherness that suggest themselves because of certain questions, issues, problems. Once I begin to define the contours of any particular subject of investigation, I will become aware of the sources I must address.

However, the second canon causes more difficulty for such selectivity. The canon of criticism is not as manageable as the canon of sources, even though it is the former tradition that influenced the formation of the canon of sources. Nevertheless, the critical tradition tends to exercise undue authority in its own time. For example, Professor Henry Hill, a University of Arizona physicist, recently gained some notoriety for his challenge to the relativity theory of Albert Einstein. Professor Hill's calculations of the sun's diameter have led him to conclude that the sun is slightly flattened at its north and south poles. If these calculations are "what really is," then Einstein's theory is wrong, say some physicists. If this is proven accurate, twentieth-century physics will change radically as a result. Those physicists who have created a world based on Einstein's theory do not take Professor Hill's challenge lightly. If he is wrong, the consequences could be devastating to his career. "A very prominent physicist told me I'd better be right," says Professor Hill, "because if I was wrong, I'd be finished in physics." This incident may be somewhat extraordinary, yet it is certainly symptomatic of the inquisitional character of much of the academic enterprise. At a time in history when freedom of critical exploration should be at its maximum, it often appears to be diminishing in the face of conventionalized authoritarianism.

In *The Heretical Imperative*, Peter Berger contrasts the religious conditions of premodern and modern humankind. Humanity is confronted with a radical pluralization that produces a condition of anxiety and doubt. The presupposed authority of a religious tradition is vanished, and with it the certainty of premodern individuals. In the premodern age, says Professor Berger, there were those who denied some aspects of a religious tradition. They were heretics because they made a choice in favor of a divergent opinion. Heresy comes from the Greek verb *hairein*—"to choose."

> In premodern situations there is a world of religious certainty, occasionally ruptured by heretical deviations. By contrast, the modern situation is a world of religious uncertainty, occasionally staved off by more or less precarious constructions of religious affirmation. Indeed, one could put this change even more sharply: For premodern man, heresy is a possibility—usually a rather remote one; for modern man, heresy typically becomes a necessity. Or again, modernity creates a new situation in which picking and choosing becomes an imperative.[6]

May it not be the case that the religious certainty of the premodern age has been transferred from the religious traditions to the traditions of academe? This kind of religious certainty is very much at home in the conventions of physical and social scientists and humanists. The heretical imperative may be a reality facing the religious traditions, but it has very little play among the ranks of critical scholars. Our selectivity of issues and of critical sources is often rigidly directed by the conventions and canons of criticism. This kind of authority needs to be challenged by the kinds of heretical moves that Berger attributes to premodern individuals. We must begin to acknowledge the existence of postmodern circumstances in which the canons of modernity are to be questioned. Heretical challenges have been hurled at the conventions of academe for some time. Some psychologists, historians, and scientists have risked their careers on behalf of the heretical imperative. But the major conclaves, partly awestruck by the marvels of applied science and somewhat comfortable in the perpetuation of manageable tasks, are largely unaffected.

Without question, every act of reading and observing influences another's reading and observing. It also affects *what* is read and observed. If I maintained that scholars who are dealing with ritual must utilize the terminology and methods of Victor Turner or Anthony F. C. Wallace, I have made a selection that will influence what I find and

---

[6]Peter Berger, *The Heretical Imperative* (Garden City: Anchor Press, 1980) 24-25.

what I report of my findings. There is also the possibility of making dishonest use of Turner and Wallace. These anthropologists, like other free scholars contemplating the encounters of otherness, come to conclusions that reflect their own particular union with the truth. If I select their terms and their methods in advance of my own contemplation, I may very well be introducing an element that influences my findings inordinately. Turner or Wallace should be consulted *after* I have done my own critical inquiry, for at that point I may wish to compare our journeys. To be sure, there are always influences brought to the task of inquiry. But that is precisely why contemplation, with its purification process, is the proper mode of inquiry.

As a critical scholar, I do not look for that which other scholars say I must look. Nor do I conduct my inquiries in the precise manner in which others have done the same task. I know that the task is possible because I have read and heard what others have said about their own inquiries. It is certainly true that I may be inspired by them and excited about taking a similar journey. In my reporting of what I have contemplated, I am forced to use common language and images. My mind is never free of ideas, words, and images that I have learned from others. However, if these "borrowings" express anything significant, if they express something of my contemplation of what really is, they point to a truth that is universally accessible. There is no plagiarism. I may, as a matter of fact, be able to fashion ideas and words that are of my own choosing. However, if I do not, and find it necessary to use the phrases and concepts of another, I am not guilty of stealing anything. What I have done is to discover that I have no better way of analyzing and expressing the object contemplated. What is more, I need not defer to the "authority" of whomever I borrow from, since whatever authority there is, may be found in what is contemplated.

As scholars of religion we have very good reasons to be selective in our use of the literature of the convention. We have limited time in which to conduct our business effectively. We ask ourselves, What is the current focus of our study; what seem to be its perimeters? If I am to search a body of evidence or ideas to learn what really is, what readings from the canons of criticism may help me in the process of purification? There may be readings the convention favors that are of no use (or of little use) in that process. They are therefore unnecessary. Whatever I read must be discardable before the face of truth, or clearly visible as an *instrument* that has participated in the creation of its own truth.

It becomes apparent that the critical inquirer must be sharply aware of his identity. He must know who he is, what his insights and presuppositions are, and where he is going. An undisciplined scholar distorts the truth without warrant. That is to say, he distorts without knowing that he is doing so, without being aware that the instruments of investigation are themselves ingredients in the discovery. The scholar's knowledge of who he is will have much to do with establishing criteria of selection. He cannot, he should not, read all there is; nor should he read or study all that the convention requires. It is he, not someone else, who is engaged in this contemplation. His personal responsibility to the convention is that he should honor the truth that his contemplation discovers and learn from it. His work is not defined by the convention, nor is he the slave of its methods.

The matter is illustrated by the process of *midrash* in the formation of Jewish thought. Midrash is the investigation that explores the principle of reality called Torah. It is the exegesis and exposition of the Torah. It seems at times a peculiar form of inquiry in that it reads and writes between the words and phrases of Scripture. It is a product of knowledge and imagination. It explores and explains between the lines. Some midrashic literature may seem exotic or far-fetched, as if it were nothing more than fantastic opinion. However, upon reflection we should begin to realize that the process depends upon *who* is doing it and what the individual brings to the process. The more effectively I have been trained by the rabbi's tradition, the more my intellect and imagination will search to find what really is. My findings may seem highly irregular to some, but that is because they have not been taught as I have; they do not bring to the process of understanding what I bring. If my education in the tradition makes me a mimic of the rabbis, saying only what they have said, using only the language of their methods, then I have not been taught well and will discover only those things that everyone expects me to discover.

Every act of study and reading is highly charged with implications. Selection is central to every such act: it determines the beginning, and often the end, of the search for knowledge and understanding. Every critical scholar must take seriously the business of selectivity. What he reads should be determined by a clear perception of who he is, what his task is, and what shall be brought to that task. His goal is to understand his influences thoroughly. By doing so, the greatest possible independence of influence will be insured, allowing the possibility of discovering what really is.

Selectivity is important because it permits time for repetition. Virtually every profound and creative scholar will have a book, a document from the canons of criticism, to which he returns again and again. No matter what the fashions of method are, we may elect to stay in loving communion with this old friend. It may be a work that is remotely related to our present subject of critical inquiry. It may be fiction like Dostoyevsky's, Melville's, or Isaac Singers's; or it may be a grand collection of essays, a work of history, philosophy, theology, or criticism. Sometimes we may not be aware of its importance. It is very likely a work that has influenced us and perhaps, through us, exerts its influence upon others.

The presence of such a work as this in the life of a scholar is not unwelcome. This may seem a curious thing to say after having posited a theory of contemplation as criticism that seeks to clarify influence and purify the critical process from all that obstructs illumination and communion with truth. However, the presence of a certain long-time companion in truth provides a different influence from that which results in employing methodology in the critical process. With a long-time companion, one has had long, sometimes loving, often stormy, dialogue. The presence of a loved one does not require constant agreement. It results in understanding, joy, and fidelity. The testimony to truth found in relationship to these documents reminds us that we are not alone in our search and informs us that the reality we discover cannot be captured for final display on the altars of human achievement.

The book or essay that is read repeatedly is an important ingredient in the contemplative process. It is important to be selective in our reading in order to have time for these old friends. They serve us as a chant serves the monk. They help us to concentrate on what is significant. They help us to trust the reality of which we are a part and which we seek to understand. They do this by centering our critical consciousness, helping us to know what is important and keeping the mind uncluttered with too many claims. We are reminded of the fact that truth is not nearly so fickle as the speculators of radical change suggest. The presence of a friend does not clutter; it accompanies. Our attention is heightened and focused because we are secure—we do not have to prove ourselves to those whose methods and conventions make claims upon us. A friend's presence consoles and reassures us, provides a rhythm to our inquiry. By the continuing presence of these important books, our minds are prepared for what will be revealed.

How is this so? I turn again to Professor Austin Farrer. In an essay reviewing Gabriel Marcel's 1951 Gifford Lectures on *The Mystery of Being*, Farrer tells us that Marcel was not gifted at systematic exposition. "He sets before us several shots or views of philosophic truth, which he labors to make vivid or penetrating." Yet Marcel does not easily state his transitions, and often "the argument gets lost in the text." What are we to do? asks Farrer. Are we to say, as some would, that Marcel's mind is defective because there is weakness of systematic unity? Not at all: the system is *there*, and "the reader may please his own vanity by writing his own account of the structure afterwards on a few sheets of paper." Contrary to prevailing belief, the structure is not nearly so important as the convention tell us. Any body of thought has structure. The time for structure may be in those moments that we are trying to clarify what has been said. But if all we produce is the structure, we have observed very little. "It is the truth of detail to which Marcel clings, because his special gift is to make us see personal and spiritual realities; he is never happy unless he is revealing something to us." We may compare Marcel and Bergson at this point, says Farrer. "A competent third-year student may write Bergson's system for him more accurately than Bergson wrote it, but who can illuminate the world as Bergson illuminated it? Tidy minds are three-a-penny, but seeing minds are rarer than fine gold. Bergson or Marcel may not present us with a philosophy, but they turn us into philosophers."[7]

This is what we want to happen. We want to be turned loose in that realm where we think the thoughts of otherness in its threefold character. A philosopher like Marcel pulls together the strands of his thought in order to communicate them to us. To do so, he must organize them. But he is interested in repeating and restating speculations in such a way that we begin to see the reality of otherness in which he and the reader both participate. His rhythm of detail is like the re-

---

[7]Austin Farrer, *Reflective Faith* (Grand Rapids: Eerdmans, 1972) 164-65.

peated reading of special books. They do not likely "present us with a philosophy, but they turn us into philosophers."

A third element in the contemplative approach to reading and study is silence. Like good shepherds, scholars have always painstakingly tended the special manuscripts and so-called primary sources. Such dedication must probably be considered a good thing. But not all contemporary scholarship is of that kind. Some of us are old enough to know scholars, good scholars, who have spent their lifetimes in continued consecration to a given problem, manuscript, author, or period. Often they "produced" little or nothing, sometimes a grand summa. But that is all changed. Now such relaxed but persevering labor would terminate a career. Today, much of our so-called scholarly effort is a seven-day-a-week, intemperate struggle to justify existence by gaining a form of salvation. It is not unlike the labors of the businessman who knows that his overexertions will gain him a larger commission, enhance his chances for promotion, and ultimately make him a millionaire—with an ulcer.

There is always one more bit of detective work to be done in the archives, more works from the canon of criticism to be honored, several reviews to be done to make certain the convention remembers you while you race against time to deliver one more offering to the altar of the profession. In all this justification by works, much of it sanctioned and demanded by the modern university (whose model is corporate industry), there is less and less time for that most valued of human experiences—silence. Contemplation is impossible without silence. The process of purification that prepares for illumination and oneness with truth cannot be done without silence.

To the contemplatives of all traditions, there is a discipline of silence that is the inner recollectedness, that stage in purification where influence is stripped naked before the truth. This standing before the truth is not simple personal choice. Rather, it is a surprise, and can only result from the silence that eventually empties us of expectations and preconceptions that keep us from seeing things as they really are. Any problem, issue, or object that causes the scholar to inquire into truth can be contemplated by surrounding it with silence. Nothing said in this essay advocates the necessity of the critical inquirer to give up his painstaking labors and analytical probes. What I appeal for is an increase in discernment, the transformation of the process of observation and intellection, so that the labors and the analysis contribute to the discovery of insight and wisdom.

Silence is essential to contemplation because we must have considerable time and space in which to view the subjects of our inquiry. The more we confront the wide range of truth in the encounters of otherness, the more we stand wide-eyed, our imaginations seeking reconstruction. We realize that the dynamic quality of otherness does not stand still for our attempts to record its momentary forms. "Our identity is a dream," writes Loren Eiseley, "we are process, not reality, for reality is an illusion of the daylight—the light of our particular day." As we inquire into such a vast, yet intimate beauty, we learn that we ourselves are part of it, that it is our business as scholars and teachers to orient ourselves to this community of otherness. We seek unity with the wholly other—the whole of otherness.

Years ago as a youth, I was a visitor to the streets and hallowed ivy precincts of Princeton, New Jersey. Like the campuses of many venerable cathedrals, colleges, and universities, Princeton is a place with a memory that is greater than the sum of all the extraordinary discoveries that have been announced by its preceptors. It is itself aesthetic testimony to the community of otherness, the truth that excites us as scholars. The day of my visit was during a vacation period. The town and its campus were quieter than usual. I walked along a tree-shaded avenue with a friend. Suddenly into the range of my vision walked a familiar figure. I had seen him many times in magazines, but I had never expected to see him so fully human, so close to me. It was like seeing a holy man. The turtleneck of his heavy sweater served like a cowl and a resting place for the shaggy gray head as he walked along, his hands behind his back. He seemed deep in thought, with little recognition of those he passed. I was profoundly impressed with the fact that I had seen Albert Einstein as a man sees his neighbor on the sidewalk. The impression has never left me. I have no idea what was going on in his mind the day that he passed. He may have been thinking of what a friend had just said to him, or the fact that he must lecture in Geneva the following week. What impressed me was the image of contemplation and the aura of silence. Perhaps none of this is evidence of anything but the structure of my own imagination. However, I cannot imagine Einstein knowing without silence and contemplation. I can certainly never see him as Ahab, only as Ishmael—in awe of the wonder he observes, and aware of the awesome responsibility that accompanies inquiry into this otherness of which we are a part.

This is the kind of understanding that came to Julian of Norwich, fourteenth-century English spiritual writer. She describes a series of visionary experiences and reflects on their meaning.

> At the same time as I saw this sight of the head bleeding, our good Lord showed a spiritual sight of his familiar love. I saw that he is to us everything which is good and comforting for our help. He is our clothing, who wraps and enfolds us for love, embraces us and shelters us, surrounds us for his love, which is so tender that he may never desert us. And so in this sight I saw that he is everything which is good, as I understand.

> And in this he showed me something small, no bigger than a hazelnut, lying in the palm of my hand, as it seemed to me, and it was as round as a ball. I looked at it with the eye of my understanding and thought: What can this be? I was amazed that it could last, for I thought that because of its littleness it would suddenly have fallen into nothing. And I was answered in my understanding. It lasts and always will, because God loves it; and thus everything has being through the love of God.[8]

How many scholars are there who are silent enough to see things as they really are, to see that the one little thing they contemplate is the wholeness of things, the truth that unites us to all things? It behooves us as scholars to cultivate the silence, or give ourselves up to the forces of technical reason that create us in their own image. Only in silence will we see things as they are. And that is what critics are supposed to do.

Of course, there is dialogue as well. In the tradition of contemplation, even the most private of persons brings his work into communication with others. He tests and is tested. He learns and he teaches. He celebrates a liturgy. The critic who accepts contemplation as the mode of personal inquiry must do the same. When we study and read, we have already acknowledged the community of inquiry by using the canons of source and the canons of critical literature. Selectivity and repetition are community activities even when done in solitude. Si-

---

[8]Julian of Norwich, *Showings* (New York: Paulist Press, 1978) 183.

lence permits our approach to understanding. Yet the preparation, the understanding, the clarification, and the communication of what we learn are aspects of community—just as what we observe is itself community.

Perhaps this element in the grammar of our contemplation is easiest to comprehend and accept. It comes closest to the practices of the convention. The guild of scholars is accustomed to sharing and exploring ideas. No school or department exists without some give-and-take among the scholars. As Rabbi Eleazar ben Arakh once lamented: "Settle in a place where Torah is studied, and do not think that it will seek you, for only your colleagues will help you hold on to it, and do not rely on your own understanding."[9] Much depends on the manner in which the dialogue is conducted. If it is done as an exercise in competition, it is meaningless because the results will fall short of seeing things as they really are. The results will be the results of competition, and hence products for the marketplace. For such "products," it *is* possible to "rely on your own understanding," because it has produced what the competition required. The truth, however, is a matter of community which questions understanding until it is transformed by the process of contemplation.

Judah Goldin expresses something of this in his commentary on a rabbinic discourse of Johanan ben Zakkai:

> The answers of the disciples are far from clear, but if we wish to capture something of the meaning of this exchange between Johanan and his disciples, it is terribly important to listen to his question with utmost attention. Johanan did not ask a trivial question, nor did he express himself carelessly. He asked about the way to which a man should "cleave," *dabaq*.

> The term *dabaq* . . . is no ordinary term, and it was no ordinary question Johanan asked, and the give-and-take with his disciples was no ordinary conversation. The idiom reveals a certain intensiveness, a certain fervor, and this is the telling thing. It is the idiom which suddenly summons up remembrances of a mood and a tone of voice. . . . As Nock wrote three decades ago: "This idea [that devotion to philosophy would make a difference in a man's life] was not thought of as a matter of purely intellectual conviction. The philosopher commonly

---

[9]Jacob Neusner, *First-Century Judaism in Crisis* (Nashville: Abingdon Press, 1975) 112.

said not 'Follow my arguments one by one, check and control them to
the best of your ability: truth should be dearer than Plato to you,' but
'Look at this picture which I paint, and can you resist its attractions?
Can you refuse a hearing to the legitimate rhetoric which I address to
you in the name of virtue?' . . . "[10]

This discussion showcases a form of dialogue that is most appropriate
to contemplation. First, it is important to recognize that dialogue ad-
dressed to truth and virtue depends on questioning. Questions free us
beyond the moment and its present understanding. Questions open us
to the dynamics of otherness and the encounter with what really is. A
question is always asked of another or others; it therefore expresses
the primacy of community. One must learn how to question and how
to listen to the question "with utmost attention."

Johanan asked about the way a man should "cleave, *dabaq*." The
cleaving was an acknowledgment of purification as an essential element in the discovery of truth. An honest question is the soul of purification; it is never trivial and never ordinary conversation. It is that
form of picture painting, to use Nock's image, that is more concerned
to join hands in the contemplation of truth than in winning an argument. This may help to explain why it is that some of the greatest insight comes to us in those lighter moments of conversation or reading,
when we are not out to make a conquest, but to ask questions. The
"lightness" of those occasions is deceptive; they are very likely the
nontrivial moments when our minds are open and questioning, rather
than on guard with advance arguments and opinions.

It is not easy to ask a question, especially when you are expected
to be (or assume that you are) an expert, an authority, a specialist.
Moreover, the modern world has taught us that this is precisely what
we must be if we are worth anything. Only authorities are asked to appear on television and are appointed to a governor's commission. Our
culture forces upon us the model of the information bank and the pur-
veyor of competitive opinions in the marketplace of ideas, proposals,
and solutions. All of this is trivia, illusion. More valuable is the person
who knows how to ask questions, who is prepared for those gracious
moments when we stand, sometimes ecstatically, sometimes sadly,

---

[10]Judah Goldin, "A Philosophical Session in a Tannaite Academy," TRADITIO 21
(1965): 13, 15.

helplessly, before the illumination of things as they really are. This is the person who finds himself at one with a wholeness, a truth, that is ever in process. Such a person is a true critic, the best of scholars.

What we read and study is best done in the contemplative manner of a Paul Elmer More:

> Regularly at four my tea is brought up. I draw the curtains, stir up the fire, turn on my reading light, and sink into silent solitary luxury. The scholar's uneasy conscience no longer worries me; I have conned all the books a man needs to know, all that are seriously worth studying, I think, and may rest, or read, as the mood takes me. Indeed, out of that background, in these seasons of repose, when one sits with foot on the fender and pipe in mouth, Plato acquires a new persuasiveness, Homer a new charm, Sophocles a new depth, Virgil a new mystery, Boswell a new humanity, and Newman a subtler grace; the Psalms take on a new grandeur and the Gospels a diviner pathos. The mechanism of life dissolves away, and the spirit forces become more substantial than the air we breathe. One begins to grow wise in place of learned.[11]

---

[11]Paul Elmer More, *Pages From an Oxford Diary* (Princeton: Princeton University Press, 1937) vol. 8, n.p.

VII / Contemplation and the Art of Teaching

I
have survived the disguise of a teacher,
dusted my clothing with chalk, spoken
to the unlistening, but for what, I want to know
now that it is ending. Why does a bittern stand
so successfully on one leg? Is this the purpose
he was formed for and as for me, dusted with chalk,
eyes not to be seen on a dark night, what was the
                    purpose
                    engendered
in me? To love, and conceal it all of my life
                    like the bittern
trying to be a reed? We are necessary failures, bird,
necessary to keep something alive that the time
                    is not ripe for.[1]

This short chapter will be a simple sermon, I think. The sermon is justified because it belongs to the art of most religious traditions. How else could one reflect on teaching without becoming somewhat of a preacher, hoping to awaken and nourish the souls of

---

[1]Loren Eiseley, "A Hider's World," *Another Kind of Autumn* (New York: Charles Scribner's Sons, 1977) 46.

those scholars who have been privileged to be interpreters and guides for struggling minds? The best that one can do is to set in relief those insights derived from contemplation that seem to apply to the role of the teacher. Of course, not all scholars are teachers, at least not in the formal sense of it. Nevertheless, one of the few occupations that affords the time and resources necessary to the support of scholarship today is the teaching profession. The private scholar or the scholar-editor is a rarity. Furthermore, there is a danger to be faced by the scholar who does not teach. He may forget that it is sometimes necessary to come out of the archives, to consider the subject closed (at least temporarily), and to tell what he has discovered. It may be a temptation to stay with the manuscripts and their interesting puzzles. But that kind of fascination is like the demonic self-righteousness that overtakes those hermits who perform sterile feats of ascetic striving for their own sake—what Berdyaev calls transcendental egoism. The scholar who withdraws into his cell and begins to bask in the light of his own self-willed delight and achievement will discover no other light but that which he took with him.

Just as the hermit must finally be responsive to those who come to his door with questions, so the scholar must be able to acknowledge some legitimate demand on his time. His wisdom must be accountable. Teaching will keep his self-will humble and his discoveries responsible to others. There is a story about one of the desert fathers, Macarius of Egypt:

> *He had heard of the austerity practiced among the fathers at Tabenna, and so journeyed fifteen days across the desert disguised as a laborer. When Macarius arrived (anonymously) at his destination, he was interviewed by the abbot and admitted on probation because he was an old man and not accustomed to rigorous abstinence like the other monks. The abbot did not want the old man to go away with a grievance. It was the beginning of Lent. Macarius observed the various activities of the brethren, "how one brother chose to fast till vespers, another for two days, another for five, how one stood up all night and sat weaving his mats all day." So Macarius proceeded to combine all these austerities in his own person.*

> *Macarius provided himself with palm-fibre ready for plaiting, took his place in a corner for the days until Easter, eating no bread and*

drinking no water, neither kneeling nor lying down, "nor sleeping nor speaking, but silently praying and efficiently plaiting, and to avoid ostentation, eating a few cabbage leaves on Sundays." The brethren were furious and complained to the abbot, asking where this inhuman creature had come from who was putting them all to shame. Either he would have to leave, or the other monks themselves would all leave. This was the first report of these austerities that had reached the abbot's ears. He pondered, praying and meditating, knowing in his heart that such things cannot be done except by one with unusual experience and discipline. And in this manner "the identity of his embarrassing visitor was . . . revealed to him." Macarius was brought to the abbot's private oratory where he was kissed and greeted by name, then gently reproached. "Why wouldst thou hide thyself from one who has longed to see you? I give thee thanks that thou has clouted the ears of these youngsters of mine, and put conceit out of them. Now, therefore, return to the place from whence thou camest: we have all been sufficiently edified by thee: and pray for us."[2]

The lesson is for Macarius as well as for the abbot's "youngsters." Their vocation is not self-willed austerity and competitive achievement. In their case, the vocation is obedience to the will of God. In the case of the scholar, it is the quest for truth, responsibility to the creative encounters of otherness. That vocation requires of us that we not forget the quest and the questions that drove us into the archives. We must come out in response to the knock on the door and we must be prepared to say what it is that we really know. We must be ready to teach, and we should take little delight in our pious compulsions.

Students in the classroom today are more prepared for instruction than for teaching. With the demise of classical and humanistic foundations in education, students come to us with little or no experience in examining the great questions and issues of life. They know no great literature, no mythology, and have had no taste of philosophy. They complain that the professor becomes too abstract, and call him a philosopher whenever he explores concepts and ideas. They have little respect for the development of ideas and think such are all equally

[2]Helen Waddell, *The Desert Fathers* (Ann Arbor: University of Michigan Press, 1957, 1977) 1-12.

valuable, equally a "matter of opinion." Professors of religion, like most humanists, are reduced to the role of instructor. They find themselves enumerating, listing, and describing basic structures and facts that are the stock-in-trade of encyclopedias and textbooks. The students dutifully copy such drivel, preparing to return the favor by faithful disgorgement of the same lists.

Of course, many scholars are satisfied with such activities because they have never learned to contemplate and to be surprised by illumination. They are part of the banality of modern scholarship and education. They are often good instructors who satisfy the mediocre expectations of their students. They are not teachers, though, because they have not discovered the supremacy of questions in the midst of contemplation. They have not gone to school with the rabbis and with Socrates.

Do we really suppose that we have introduced students to religion when they leave our classrooms having listed the basic teachings and historical data that comprise a given tradition or set of traditions? Our answer will be in the affirmative if those are the perimeters of our own understanding. However, no one who has known the art of contemplation as a key to critical inquiry will be satisfied with such limited vision. He will know that teaching is an art distinct from the technique of instruction. He understands that the dynamic character of otherness in which we live and move and have our being is only understood in contemplation, and that teaching is the art of preparing for that discovery. The traditions and their history acquire vitality and validity as *religious* phenomena only if seen through contemplation.

The teaching of religious studies is an act of communication that enables the student to see how religious traditions made ultimate sense of the universe. They will not gain that understanding without first being shown how to do the kind of thinking that is concerned with making ultimate sense of the universe. For these insights into our task, I am indebted to a little-known work by Clement W. Welsh.[3] Welsh reminds us that as teachers we are dealing with people who are not accustomed to thinking as religion thinks. Most people have very little experience in trying to make ultimate sense of the universe. Before

---

[3]Clement W. Welsh, *Preaching in a New Key* (Philadelphia: Pilgrim Press, 1974) passim.

they can learn how religions make their unique response to the encounters of otherness, they must first be made aware of such encounters and shown how humans respond to them. It does no good to speak of Shariah, of Torah, or of Gospel, if the student has no experience with what it is that a gospel might do. If we speak of the ascetic sensibilities of Muhammad that led to his withdrawal to the mountains where the call to recite the revelation took place, we often encourage students to deal with remote and often bizarre experiences that "some people used to believe." Without *experience* in making ultimate sense of the universe, the notion of asceticism is trivial and boring; and the idea of revelation is far-fetched and pathological. Regrettably, we often teach paramnesiacs. Language about revelation, symbols, laws, and ritual acts are part of a medium for which many students have no memory.

Our teaching is dishonest in that the phenomena we examine and list are the products of those who *have had experience* in making ultimate sense of the universe. They are phenomena that cannot be understood except in those circumstances. Only renewed attention to the art of contemplation in teaching will eliminate the dishonesty. There seems to be little likelihood of understanding religion without learning to think religiously. I should like to suggest that this way of thinking must be taught using contemplation because it goes against the stream of much contemporary assumption. Both inside and outside academe we are enamored with what Paul Elmer More called the "demon of the absolute," which is simply "reason run amuck." More claims that:

> Reason, so long as it is content to accept the actual data of experience, is manifestly one of our diviner faculties; at every step in life it is our guide and friend, and without it we can do nothing wisely or prosperously. And that is why it becomes so dangerous when, disregarding "matters of fact, those unconcerning things," it sets up its own absolutes as the truth and asks us to act thereupon. For there are no absolutes in nature; they are phantoms created by reason itself in its own likeness, delusions which, when once evoked, usurp the field of reality and bring endless confusion in their train.[4]

---

[4]Paul Elmer More, *The Demon of the Absolute* (Princeton: Princeton University Press, 1928) 1-2.

This usurpation by reason is a constant activity, creating its confusion in politics, religion, and in most of the emerging academic disciplines. Reason demands a monism that the world of nature does not admit. Reason says "it must be so," and creates absolute states and absolute gods. The result is that one has difficulty reconciling the data of experience to these "absolutes." In theology, for example, the creator of the absolute God tries desperately to reconcile the idiosyncrasies of human suffering with the honor of God's omnipotent being. The ineffable and infinite absolute of certain mystical systems requires its creators to declare themselves illusions so that they might be dissolved into its own ineffable morass.

The study of religions demonstrates to us that, in fact, the data of experience is more than our religious rationalism. There must be a mode of thinking that is able to maintain the balance that is destroyed when reason decides to exploit one human insight into an absolute. That mode of thinking is contemplation, and it is the heart of what the religion scholar must learn to teach. Human beings are creatures who have developed to a high degree the ability to receive sense perceptions from the environment, use them, and return others back into the environment. The "growth" we demonstrate as humans will be in proportion to our ability to advance this process effectively. We must be able to maintain the stability of our openness to encounters with the environment, the integrity required to bring them to conscious effect, and the need to return some of those effects and their waste products to the larger environment.

Human beings experience these metabolic relationships as encounters with otherness. There is a personal and conscious element to all these encounters, even when they are pursued as scientific enterprises. This is what accounts for the narrative form in most of our attempts to communicate our experience. We "report" our "findings," "tell" about them. Much of what is significant in our stories concerns the encounters of otherness, which are most effectively observed and understood by way of contemplation. They do not really "sit still" for anything other than contemplation. Storytelling is the form of communication that most adequately helps us to speak of things as they really are. The best thinking is that which results in the greatest story. Growth is demonstrated by the ability of story-thinking to include ever-greater perceptions from the environment, without following the inordinate demands of reason for an absolute solution.

The wise teacher will seek to have students expand the stories of their own existence in order to understand more effectively those great stories that are the traditions of human religiousness. The teacher's role will be similar to that of the fool in many of these traditions. It is as much the teacher's function to stand things on their heads as it is to provide information. The teacher must do the mad things that suggest the possibility of the impossible. However, the madness must come easily; it may not be feigned and, therefore, be too contrived or phony to the students. There is a kind of madness that results from seeing things as they really are; a gift of madness that makes the good teacher one who shatters the composure and ordinary expectations of students.

The teacher is rather like the Mad Hatter of *Alice in Wonderland*. After having posed a number of riddles without answers (perhaps demonstrating the importance of questions), he incurs the wrath of the frustrated Alice: "I think you might do something better with the time," she said, "than wasting it in asking riddles that have no answers."

"If you knew Time as well as I do," said the Hatter, "you wouldn't talk about wasting *it*. It's *him*."

"I don't know what you mean," said Alice.

"Of course you don't!" the Hatter said, tossing his head contemptuously. "I dare say you never even spoke to Time!"

"Perhaps not," Alice cautiously replied, "but I know I have to beat time when I learn music."

"Ah! That accounts for it," said the Hatter. "He won't stand beating."[5]

Teachers wishing to break through the ossifications of time that are part of contemporary society will find themselves being the fool, a Mad Hatter forcing those situations in which a student may encounter the possibility of the sacredness and personality of time. The task is a difficult one, and professors of religion will discover that most of

---

[5]Lewis Carroll, *Alice's Adventures in Wonderland and Through the Looking Glass* (London: Collier-Macmillan, Ltd., 1962, 1969) 90.

their students are imprisoned within a realm of ordinary rationality that accepts as absolute the routinization of time.

The fools of the great traditions often renounced what others regarded as sanity and mental balance. Audacious and humble at the same time, they awakened people from complacency and self-satisfaction through startling deeds or enigmatic statements. Through their detachment from customary expectations, they released certain responses in others that stimulated the subconscious and led thereby to the purification essential to insight and illumination. Most teachers may not be able to extend themselves to the extremes of such madness, but if they would be effective and be more than purveyors of information, they must be prepared to risk madness.

The Sufi tradition of Islam is replete with the madcap episodes of such fools as Nasrudin and Abu Yazid. On one occasion the latter saint was greeted by throngs from his hometown as he returned from a pilgrimage to the holy city of Medina. It was the month of Ramadan, during which Muslims are obliged to fast. As the people approached him, Abu Yazid "pulled out a loaf of bread and defiantly devoured it before their astonished eyes. The crowd shrank away in horror and disgust." The pilgrimage is also one of the five pillars, or essential practices, of Islam. On one occasion, Abu Yazid was asked by a stranger whom he encountered on the road, "Where are you going?"

"On the pilgrimage," replied Abu Yazid.

"How much have you got?"

"Two hundred dirhams."

"Come, give them to me," the man demanded. "I am a man with a family. Circle round *me* seven times. That is your pilgrimage."

"I did so," said Abu Yazid, "and returned home."[6]

The story that most impresses me with its understanding of the the teacher as a fool is told by Elie Wiesel in his collection of Hasidic portraits and tales, *Souls on Fire.*

In a faraway land a prince lost his mind and imagined he was a rooster. He took to living under a table, naked, refusing the luscious delicacies from the royal kitchen and insisting on the grain reserved for the rooster. The king was beside himself. He summoned all kinds of physi-

---

⁶Richard C. Martin, *Islam* (Englewood Cliffs: Prentice-Hall, Inc., 1982) 66-67.

cians and specialists, all of whom admitted their inability to deal with the prince. Magicians, monks, miracle-workers—all their efforts were in vain.

One day an unknown sage presented himself at court. "I think that I could heal the prince," he said shyly. "Will you allow me to try?"

The king consented, and to the surprise of all present, the sage removed his clothes, and joining the prince under the table, began to crow like a rooster.

Suspicious, the prince interrogated him: "Who are you and what are you doing here?" "And you," replied the sage, "who are you and what are you doing here?" "Can't you see? I am a rooster!" "Hmm," said the sage, "how very strange to meet you here!" "Why strange?" "You mean, you don't see? Really not? You don't see that I'm a rooster just like you?"

The two men became friends and swore never to leave each other.

And the sage undertook to cure the prince by using himself as example. He started by putting on a shirt. The prince couldn't believe his eyes. "Are you crazy? Are you forgetting who you are? You really want to be a man?" "You know," said the sage in a gentle voice, "you mustn't ever believe that a rooster who dresses like a man ceases to be a rooster." The prince had to agree. The next day both dressed in the normal way. The sage sent for some dishes from the palace kitchen. "Wretch! What are you doing?" protested the prince, frightened in the extreme. "Are you going to eat like them now?" His friend allayed his fears: "Don't ever think that by eating like man, with man, at his table, a rooster ceases to be what he is; you mustn't ever believe that it is enough for a rooster to behave like a man to become human; you can do anything with man, in his world and even for him, and yet remain the rooster you are."

And the prince was convinced; he resumed his life as a prince.[7]

The sage was indeed an astute critic who saw things as they really are, and was able to demonstrate, to *teach*, the nature of reality by an act of personal madness. He was a fool; and, of course, only sages can be fools. In a world wherein sanity produces some of our most inhumane experiences, we have more evidence than ever for the need of a fool to help us work our way through the madness of our presumed sanity. As Thomas Merton pointed out: "We can no longer assume that because

[7]Elie Wiesel, *Souls on Fire* (New York: Vintage Books, 1972) 170-71.

a man is 'sane' he is therefore in his 'right mind,' "[8] Aldolf Eichmann was pronounced "perfectly sane." It is the same assumed sanity that pervades modern scholarship, which struggles to avoid the search for truth as it seeks to extinguish those who do not agree with its beliefs and practices. Only a teacher who knows he must reject this sanity becomes a guide to the encounter of things as they really are, restoring the health of society. "Among physicians and priests," wrote R. D. Laing, "there should be some who are guides, who can educt the person from this world and induct him to the other."[9]

All of which reminds us that the role of teacher is also that of guide—the imitator of the saints, and a guide to the necessity of discipline. The entire academic process today, with its emphasis upon functional training and specialization, has little time for remembering that there is truth, that it must be pursued in a certain manner, that there are those whose lives are exemplary to the search. As Plato says in the Theaetetus: "God is never in any wise unjust, but most perfectly just, and there is nothing more like to Him than one of us who should make himself just to the limit of man's power." The human race seems easily deprived of its memory. We are readily able to proceed in life as if others did not really exist except as the objects of our manipulation. It is easy to forget that we live in encounter with an inexhaustible otherness, the whole of which is the source of our very being and consciousness. We live as though we had not been created in this image in order to reflect its likeness—"there is nothing more like to Him than one of us who should make himself just to the limit of man's power."

In the archives, the laboratory, and the classroom, as well as in the marketplace, we deny or forget this fundamental fact of our existence.

> *When there is no temple there shall be no homes,*
> *Though you have shelters and institutions,*
> *Precarious lodgings while the rent is paid,*
> *Subsiding basements where the rat breeds*
> *Or sanitary dwellings with numbered doors*
> *Or a house a little better than your neighbor's;*
> *When the Stranger says: "What is the meaning of this city*

---

[8]Thomas Merton, *Thomas Merton on Peace* (New York: McCall Publishing Co., 1971) 161.

[9]Quoted in Kenneth Leech, *Soul Friend* (San Francisco: Harper & Row, 1978) 109.

> *Do you huddle close together because you love each other?"*
> *What will you answer? "We all dwell together*
> *To make money from each other"? or "This is a community"?*[10]

I recall the first time I read Eliot's words; I burst out laughing. I had never really pondered the absurdity of our civilization. Imagine, if you will, human beings possessed of immense consciousness and intelligence, using that potential in the singularly inane business of making money from each other. This is parabolic of the academic world as well, not only in its competitive race to do those things required by the corporate mentality as proof of merit for promotion, tenure, and salary increments, but also in the use of conventions whereby we seek to impress each other by the sum of our footnotes.

It is the responsibility of the teacher to guide students in the proper use of memory and intelligence. This mandate assumes that professors are themselves aware of these qualities, that they understand their relationship to the realities they study. They must first remember that they are in quest of what really is, that they are children of and in encounter with the realms of otherness that sustain our consciousness. The teacher must be a pilgrim in search of truth, not a technician who seeks to make money or to fashion the world that money fantasizes.

It is not easy to be a guide. However, the good teacher knows the lives of the saints, whose quest for truth was exemplary. He knows the paths to the discovery of what really is, and the discipline required to follow that path. However, his students are products of a culture that has lost the memory of truth. Their culture is dedicated to utility, accompanied by a homogenization of opinion. The student tends to believe that all opinions are of equal value, instead of realizing that all opinions are merely politically acceptable. If you would educate students, you must guide them to the point where they discover that their assumptions are not true, and begin to employ the discipline that is necessary to the pursuit of truth.

The faculty of the human spirit that responds to the claims of truth is very likely present in all of us, but we often have little memory of it and frequently little time for it. The activity of that spirit makes steady

---

[10]T. S. Eliot, "Choruses from 'The Rock'," *The Complete Poems and Plays, 1909-1950* (New York: Harcourt, Brace, and Co., 1952) 103.

choices among our ordinary inclinations and demands the purification mentioned earlier. It comes into its own only by a discipline that is at first agonizing and offensive to many of us. By nature we are inclined to grasp at the nearest and easiest opinion or experience, to make light of the discipline someone may suggest is necessary to adequate understanding. The good teacher will be like Ishmael, who deems it "well to be on friendly terms with *all* the inmates of the place one lodges in," whose motives are a contagion that makes us follow him to the point where "the great flood-gates of the wonder-world swung open, and in the wild conceits that swayed me to my purpose, two and two there floated into my inmost soul, endless processions of the whale, and, mid most of them all, one grand hooded phantom, like a snow hill in the air."[11]

Ahab always rages about for conquest and vengeance. He is a person of strong opinions, easily exercised by a moment's discussion or a threat (veiled or unveiled) to the natural inclination for supremacy. Conversely, Ishmael is the person of wonder who guides others into the same pathways. The teacher does not confirm the student's tendency to cling to natural inclinations, nor the student's preference for easy opinions and pleasures. Instead, the teacher introduces the student to ideas and examples that at first may be painful to consider. As a teacher of religion, he wants the student to encounter the *more than* in the midst of existence that has accounted for the religious traditions of the world and most of the great artistic expressions of history. Without that encounter, there is no understanding.

Education is the ability to wonder and to evaluate. The educated person is the one who has contemplated things as they really are. This person has become a true critic, one who has the right to pronounce on standards of taste and of meaning because he or she has been guided into the discipline of knowing and wondering. The educated person has discovered that questions and answers are never matters of easy opinion, that there are higher and lower tastes, pleasures, and opinions. This discovery does not mean that he becomes a snob before the common affairs of the race. In fact, the educated person sees them for what they are, in a new light—one in which they no longer belong to some particular party or representative other. Because con-

---

[11]Herman Melville, *Moby Dick* (New York: Modern Library, 1950) 6.

templation has enabled the learned individual to see things as they really are, he is freed from the limitations that confine the values of otherness to their singular or representative forms. The educated person does not say: "That is a common, vulgar, folk-tale; it is inferior to the refined, cultured ideas of philosophers and persons of letters." By personal contemplation such a person observes a transformation of those so-called common forms, so that they may become instances of rare insight and illumination. That which is common and that which is refined both share the potential for truth. Yet only the person of wisdom has the perspective to understand this. Such individuals may be readers of Zane Grey, mystery stories, and romantic thrillers, as well as of the classics. If so, it is because they have been taught and shown a widened horizon that sets them free from narrow-mindedness. Things are seen as those things really are, each in its time and degree, but always in relationship to the otherness that is our common heritage of truth.

VIII / Contemplation
and the
Making of Many Books

Besides being wise, the Preacher also taught the people knowledge, weighing and studying and arranging proverbs with great care. The Preacher sought to find pleasing words, and uprightly he wrote words of truth.

The sayings of the wise are like goads, and like nails firmly fixed are the collected sayings which are given by one Shepherd. My son, beware of anything beyond these. Of making many books there is no end, and much study is a weariness to the flesh.[1]

It is true, of course. What is most difficult to comprehend is how it could have been so in the days of the author of Ecclesiastes. Why is it that humans have sought to leave so many scribblings and scratchings for others to see? Long before the invention of printing, there were those who decided that certain utterances were so important that they must be studied and copied for others to read. When it became evident that one could preserve ideas and make memories by pressing many symbols into parchment and leather, the process of book-making became a feverish affair. Soon the making of books was a matter of honor and of devotion, and then a business too impulsive to stop. It is one thing, says the editor who reflects on the sage of Ecclesiastes, for a teacher (preacher) to find the words to communicate

---

[1] Ecclesiastes 12:9-12 (RSV).

truth and wisdom; it is quite another to be swept into this prideful enterprise that makes one a weary slave to the flesh. How well he describes the plight of the twentieth-century scholar!

The making of many books has accelerated beyond belief since the days of the writing of Ecclesiastes in third century, B.C.E. There was once a time, not very long ago, when those who wrote books were persons who *wanted* to write, or had a particular flair for the written word. Now, it is demanded that a university scholar be a regular participant in publishing. The religion scholar is no different from others in this regard. The moral problem facing the scholar who must publish is not the matter of slavery to a prideful enterprise. Today's scholar acknowledges little morality in knowledge or in scholarship. But sooner or later we must face the fact that proliferation has contributed to the prostitution of language.

As teachers, scholars are responsible for the sacredness of words. They are responsible for what they see. Before they write many words to make many books, scholars are confronted with the sinfulness of their actions. Is such writing justifiable? Each decision is an important one.

A. J. Heschel tells the story of Rabbi Isaac Meir Alter of Ger, famous Talmudic scholar in Poland. One day he went to visit his master, asking him to evaluate a commentary he had written on Hoshen Mishpat, the Jewish civil code. Rabbi Mendel of Kotzk examined the writing very carefully and several weeks later summoned the author to his study. "My son, I have studied your manuscript," he said to Isaac Meir. "It is a work of genius. When it is published, the classical commentaries, which have been studied for generations, will become obsolete. I am only grieved at the thought of the displeasure this will cause to the souls of the saintly commentators." It was a winter evening. Fire was burning in the stove. Rabbi Isaac Meir took his manuscript from the table and threw it into the flames.[2]

Seemingly an act of professional lunacy we would conclude. The considerations, the premises on which the decision was made, are foreign to us. At best, we would assume that a humility inappropriate to

---

[2]Abraham Joshua Heschel, *The Earth is the Lord's* (New York: Farrar Straus Giroux, 1978) 93-94.

scholarship was at work. Perhaps the story is more hagiographical than reportorial. Even so, it directs our attention to issues that should be considered in these days of conventionalized academic publishing. One has a responsibility to the community of sages who have contemplated the truth through the centuries. "It is a work of genius," said Rabbi Mendel; but genius by itself does not represent a greater approximation of truth. Genius may lead to the manipulation of methods and ideas for the sake of demonstrating its own virtues. Perhaps the work of genius has been done without contemplation of things as they really are. If there is no concern for the tradition in which truth has found expression, there is likely to be little truth in the work of genius.

The making of many books is not *necessarily* a good thing. There is an ethic of publication that derives from the art of contemplation itself. Before we consider certain elements in such a grammar (or ethic), it is probably well to remind ourselves of the mystery of words that is at the heart of our concern for writing and publishing. Deep in our unconscious is the memory of the words that called us into being, the words that raised human existence out of the course of nature and began the process of civilization. We know, without being consciously aware of it, that all we are and know exists because of words. It is empirically true that nothing exists without Adam's naming: without the words there is nothing.

"Children trust in language," writes N. Scott Momaday. "They are open to the power and beauty of language, and here they differ from their elders, most of whom have come to imagine that they have found words out, and so much of [the] magic is lost upon them."[3] It is part of the sophistication of this age of technical reason that we assume we "have found words out"; so we abuse them and trivialize them. But their sacredness plays its magic upon us in curious ways. Somehow, we hope that in spite of the writing of many books, we have participated in the most supreme act of creation when we have set our words down.

> I wonder at the words, *What are they?* They stand, they lean and run upon the page of a manuscript—I have made a manuscript, rude and illustrious. The page bears the likeness of a boy—so simply crude the

---

[3]N. Scott Momaday, *The Names* (New York: Harper and Row, 1976) 92.

likeness to some pallid shadow on my blood—and his name consists in the letters there, the words, the other likeness, the little jumbled drawings of a ritual, the nominal ceremony in which all homage is returned, the legend of the boy's having been, of his going on. I have said it; I have set it down. I trace the words; I touch myself to the words, and they stand for me. My mind lives among them, moving ever, ever going on.[4]

There is something like that passionate wonderment in each of us as we stand, like Momaday and Ishmael, before something that is part of us, identifying us, reciting our awareness of ourselves. Words are the windows of otherness. They are those transparent and reflective realities that take us back to the moment when everything that exists came into being in the awareness of humans, the moment "when man acquired 'otherness,' when he left the safe confines of the . . . world of animals"[5] in order to name them all, including himself. But it is the writing of those words that makes the difference. The writing makes it possible to *see* the words, to see the reality of otherness in them, to identify with them, and (what is most important) to *remember*. Written words alert us to the passage of time and place. They put us in touch with moments before consciousness when we stood ready to encounter otherness in its singular, representative, and wholly other formations.

Comparing human emergence with the intelligence of porpoises, Loren Eiseley points to the importance of hands in the human saga. Without hands,

> our thoughts . . . will be as limited as those of the first men who roved in little bands in the times before fire and the writing that was to open to man the great doorway of his past. Man without writing cannot long retain his history in his head. His intelligence permits him to grasp some kind of succession of generations; but without writing, the tale of the past rapidly degenerates into fumbling myth and fable. Man's greatest epic, his four long battles with the advancing ice of the great continental glaciers, has vanished from human memory without a trace. Our illiterate fathers disappeared and with them, in a few scant generations, died one of the greatest stories of all time. This episode

---

[4]Ibid., 93.

[5]Loren Eiseley, *The Night Country* (New York: Charles Scribner's Sons, 1971) 221.

has nothing to do with the biological quality of a brain between then and now. It has to do instead with a device, an invention made possible by the hand.[6]

That invention was the written word. Those of us who spend a lifetime trying to understand the journeys of the mind do much of our work by virtue of that invention. We contemplate the otherness in which we participate. We analyze and construct in order to be good critics, good scholars. We wish to see things as they really are, and we hope to tell what we have seen. At least we hope to *come close* to telling what we have seen. Our contemplation and our telling are escapades among written words. We are primal man and modern man, all in a moment. Each generation receives a little capsule of instructions, says Eiseley, that passes through the eye of a needle like a blowing seed. They are carried "through the molecular darkness of a minute world below the field of human vision and of time's decay." The instructions will fashion, by way of their own code and alphabet, the individuals of succeeding generations. The same is true of those social structures called civilizations.

> They are transmitted from one generation to another in invisible puffs of air known as words—words that can also be symbolically incised on clay. As the delicate printing on the mud at the water's edge retraces a visit of autumn birds long since departed, so the little tablets in perished cities carry the seeds of human thought across the deserts of millennia.[7]

Writing is so important to the art of criticism as contemplation that it is very difficult to know what led Rabbi Isaac Meir to throw his manuscript—"a work of genius"—into the flames. Yet there are ethical concerns to be considered. We must be responsible writers. First, we remind ourselves that the writing and publication habits of the contemporary academician are the result of mandates derived from the models of technology and corporate industry. Such writing has little concern for the quality of words. It is unaware of the power and authority of the word and would probably label the ideas of Loren Eiseley

---

[6]Loren Eiseley, *The Star Thrower* (New York: Harcourt-Brace Jovanovich, Inc., 1978) 41.

[7]Ibid., 123.

"mystification." Today's colleges and universities have been possessed by technical and corporate reason and methods. Consumerism has become a standard for the role and procedures of higher education, affecting its teaching and its scholarship. In technology and business it is important to make quantitative evaluation of one's effectiveness. Technique, functionality, and management are basic criteria. One questions the manner in which these criteria have achieved hegemony in higher education. The obvious answer is that they are the hallmarks of our culture, and are therefore to be expected in the university. Nevertheless, it is hoped that the university will maintain a respectable prophetic distance from the culture of a given historical moment. This, of course, is precisely the point of difficulty for the contemporary university, which is increasingly under the control of the state and subservient to business and high technology.

Those scholars called humanists, who rummage among the words, ideas, and events of history, are ill-advised to respond to the criteria of technique, functionality, and management. It is a distortion of scholarship for the university to demand the application of those criteria. That a humanistic scholar would be confronted with administrative requests for evidence of time and stress management is an imposition of subversive proportions. To be asked by a committee of peers, who reflect the views of an already submissive administration, to give evidence of a long-range research plan is tantamount to being told that the company will fail unless the employees demonstrate continuing contribution to produce improvement or new-product development. Humanists, whether in science or letters, do not "do research," nor should they demean their scholarly study, investigation, and writing by calling it that.

The results of technological and business research can readily be "written up" in easy and successive installments. It is logical to their purposes and methods to do such reporting on the basis of a long-range sequence of planned troubleshooting. Scholars of religion have become conventionalized by this model of reportorial writing. Of course, the humanist can play the game, too. He can respond to the expectation of long-range "research plans" and regular "write-ups" by immersing himself in the methods that are so basic to technology and business. He can report on the applicability of method to the workings of ideas and words that have previously seemed to ignore "method." Or he can deal with methodology itself. The results of his work will appear to be highly complex and will meet the criteria of the system.

If we must continue to conform to the models of technology and business, let us do just that. Let us devise journals that permit *brief* reports on "research" and "method," thereby fulfilling the requirement for sustained "productivity." But let us devote our honest time to contemplation, to the study and understanding of things as they really are; and let us write with reverence for words. Reportorial research is an affair of management and productivity. Writing is a literary event and should be an affair of the soul.

Recently I have heard of several religion scholars who have "ruined their careers" by publishing literary works. They have published what was *not* reportorial in a journal or book that was unacceptable to the convention. Perhaps we are no longer scholars and persons of letters, but simply "religious engineers." It should begin to be evident to us, however, that we are no longer dealing with the heart of religion; nor are we contemplating the truth.

This book is a plea for a return to letters, to artistry. To write about religion is to work with the secret of words; it is a literary task, not an exercise in reporting. Until we make this transition, we are faced with the making of many books that are "much ado about nothing."

In Isaac Singer's story "The Plagiarist," the rabbi of Machlev ponders the matter of publishing and remembers the words of his grandfather:

> *It is written in Psalms that when the Messiah comes, "Then shall all the trees of the wood rejoice." The question that arises is: Why should the trees rejoice? What concern is it of theirs? The answer is that by the time the Messiah arrives, authors will have written so many volumes that books will supply the necessary fuel for stoves. Thus there will no longer be any need to burn wood, and the trees will rejoice at having been spared.*[8]

One frequently gets the impression that it must be close to the time of the Messiah's coming.

There are, of course, occasions when it is essential for the scholar to write. Not as an occasion of reporting to meet the testing criteria of

---

[8]Isaac B. Singer, *The Seance* (New York: Fawcett Crest, 1981) 92.

an academic promotions, tenure, and salary adjustments committee, but as an act of integrity. Professor Eiseley writes in his autobiography about the scholar's temptation to a certain ascetic smugness. He struggled against these seductions in the course of his investigations into the work of Charles Darwin.[9] First, there was the "phobia of incompleteness," the sense that nothing could be committed to writing until every conceivable source and document had been consulted. It is easy to ignore the fact that what one has contemplated and begun to understand may never again be encountered in quite the unique configurations of the present moment. That is, the scholar may begin to assume that he is virtually immortal, and can assimilate *every* detail without any sense of limitation. He refuses to write because he feels there is more to contemplate, to investigate; and he has a fear of being premature, incomplete. He does not wish to risk the ridicule of the convention or compromise some private code of integrity. "So great is the lure of documents, however, that it is easy to be lulled into a false sense of omnipotence." We learn from contemplation that the truth we pursue is *always* in some sense more than its expression; yet it lends itself to communication by word. This means that no writing can pretend to be equivalent to the truth as absolute. Still, good and responsible writing will be a vehicle for the truth as otherness.

Eiseley suggests that, as a part of this ascetic retreat, there is frequently the feeling that "publishing comes to seem a heresy." One is in the presence of so holy and precious an experience that the desire to nurture and prolong the experience is overwhelming. Why leave the vaults, the jungle, the excavations? Who else could possibly understand the holiness? Perhaps there is not time to commit to writing what must inevitably be cheapened and lessened by words. Scholars of religious contemplation recognize this as the most insidious of human temptations and sins. The *acquisition* of "experience" is the beginner's fallacy; it is the story of Adam and Eve, the glittering fantasy of the apple in the midst of the Garden. The sensible scholar, experienced as a contemplative critic, knows that there is a time to brush off the dust of the archives and set things on paper. He is prepared to say what is necessary to say. He knows that all things are set in relations

---

[9]The following account is from Loren Eiseley, *All the Strange Hours* (New York: Charles Scribner's Sons, 1975) 184-87.

and that illumination is a gift to the person who has no great illusion about his findings. "The world as experience," wrote Martin Buber, "belongs to the basic word I-It. The basic word I-You establishes the world of relation."[10]

We simply write, therefore, because the finding demands it, so long as we have no absolute predictions of the worth of the results. Since all things exist in relations, the words we write must tell the best possible story. If they make too great a claim on the truth, they will attempt to bracket, to objectify, and in so doing depart from the only truth there is—the illuminations of things as they really are in their otherness.

Buber tells the story of the disciple who wrote down all the teachings he had heard from the Baal Shem Tov, beloved founder of modern Hasidism. One day the Baal Shem saw a demon going through the house, carrying a book in his hand. "What book is that?" asked the Baal Shem. "That is the book," said the demon, "of which you are the author."

The Baal Shem called all his people together. He knew that someone had been secretly setting down in writing the things he said. "Who of you," he asked, "is writing down what I teach you?" The disciple in question readily admitted what he had been doing and brought the results to his master. The Baal Shem studied it for a long time, page after page. "In all this," he said, "there is not a single word I said. You were not listening for the sake of Heaven, and so the power of evil used you for its sheath, and your ears heard what I did not say."[11]

Listening "for the sake of Heaven" is remembering that what one studies is like a foretaste. It is never final nor absolute. There is always more to the relations of otherness. So one is content to write without delusions of grandeur.

The world's religious traditions have undersides that are considered esoteric. These undersides are often subcultures, the traditions as they are known and practiced by a distinct minority. They came into being because there are persons who question the claims made for ordinary explanations and routine practices. These persons search for

---

[10]Martin Buber, *I and Thou* (New York: Charles Scribner's Sons, 1970) 56.

[11]Martin Buber, *Tales of the Hasidim: The Early Masters* (New York: Schocken Books, 1947, 1972) 66.

and point to maximal dimensions in the tradition. They realize that the knowledge that produced the tradition in the first place was of greater power than that which is realized by ordinary practitioners. They realize also that all symbolic power is greater than our momentary understanding of it. A scriptural text, an icon, a prayer, a ritual act—each is always more powerful than the explanations that either scholars or followers can describe. The pursuit of the deeper truth, the additional or maximal meaning, leads to the formation of a special knowledge and practice, a *way* that represents the profound underside of the religious tradition—be it Christian, Jewish or Buddhist.

There are those who would maintain that this profound underside represents the original form of faith and practice. It is the deposit from the time before the tradition became a public religion. These maximal ways deal with the reality of the *more than* that is fundamental to every human encounter. This accounts for the fact that adherents of a maximal way often tend to be derisive of ordinary scholarship.

The maximal way of Islam is generally known as Sufism. From this way comes the familiar story of Ajmal Hussein, who was forever being criticized by scholars who sought to cast doubts upon his knowledge and who accused him of hiding behind mysticism to avoid answering their criticisms. "If I answer my critics," said Ajmal,

> *they make it the opportunity to bring fresh accusations against me, which people believe because it amuses them to believe such things. If I do not answer them they crow and preen themselves, and people believe that they are real scholars. They imagine that we Sufis oppose scholarship. We do not. But our very existence is a threat to the pretended scholarship of tiny noisy ones. Scholarship long since disappeared. What we have to face now is sham scholarship.*

At this pronouncement of Ajmal, the scholars scoffed more loudly than ever. So Ajmal decided to demonstrate his point. He invited the scholars to test him with "question papers." Fifty professors and academicians sent papers; Ajmal answered each one differently. The scholars met at a conference to discuss the papers and there were so many versions of what Ajmal believed that each questioner believed that it was his question which exposed Ajmal. The result was the celebrated "brawling of the scholars." For five days they attacked each other bitterly.

This [said Ajmal] is a demonstration. What matters to each one most is his own opinion and his own interpretation. They care nothing for truth. This is what they do with everyone's teachings. When he is alive, they torment him. When he dies they become experts on his works. The real motive of the activity, however, is to vie with one another and to oppose anyone outside their own ranks. Do you want to become one of them? Make a choice soon. [12]

What the maximal ways teach us is that scholarship is constantly tempted to lose its contemplative commitment, with the result being a necessary attachment to arguments, findings, and interpretations. This is why virtually every maximal way will point to the goal of detachment. The truth is not something one possesses; it is always a present relationship to a maximal reality that is obviously greater than its momentary realization. This, of course, is simply another way of regarding existence as an affair of singular, representative, and wholly otherness. The difference between Ajmal and the scholars may be a vocational one, but it would not be nearly so violent a relationship if the scholars were contemplative.

The scholar writes because his findings demand it, because the word needs saying—because the written word is itself truth, a way of remembering, a way of communicating with the timeless character of otherness in which we exist as humans. One must record what one sees, feels, knows, and remembers. Freedom is important. If I have taken the responsibility for writing, the process of publication should not be impeded by the conventions of referees. This, of course, is heresy. Refereeing of journals, and to some extent, of books has no doubt contributed to the standardization of predefined excellence. But the guilds are slow to admit those whose arguments, methods, and styles are somewhat irregular. Footnotes must stand the test of profusion and show the evidence of proper editions and original sources, even when such standards may be somewhat irrelevant to the scholar's writing. In what may be the most presumptuous of all expectations, the referee seeks the references to his own writings and those of other members of the convention. This is understandable, and essential to the main-

---

[12]Indries Shah, *Wisdom of the Idiots* (New York: E. P. Dutton, 1971) 51-52.

tenance of the conventional wisdom. But the referee can be heady with power and refuse to read the words *for the virtue of their own intention.*

Editors need to follow their own hearts and minds much more than they have in the recent past. If a manuscript does a masterful job of achieving its intent and communicates one scholar's experience to the minds of people, it should probably be published. Otherwise, refereeing will eventually lead to the publication of disparate offerings that represent the miserly *pilpul* of a conventional elite.

The humanistic scholar must maintain integrity in his writing. When it is time for him to do so, he should write about what he has discovered in the manner that is appropriate to him. He is not a member of a laboratory staff, charged with contributing his sets of data and interpretation to the prearranged program of methods, materials, and terminology of the laboratory.

In Isaac Singer's story, "The Mirror," there is an imp who tries to seduce a beautiful woman. "The writers of books," he says, "have the brains of a flea: they merely parrot each other."[13] It is not always so, of course. And the imp was twisting the wisdom toward a selfish and ill-begotten end. Nevertheless, he reminds us that much of the writing of the refereeing and conventional elite is parroting.

There is a problem for the contemplative scholar in our age; it "lies in sustaining the air flight of the superior intellect above the necessary ruts it is forced to travel. As Thoreau comments, the heel of the true author wears out no road. 'A thinker's weight is in his thought, not in his tread.' "[14] There is a repression that is the mark of our times, a repression that fears the unique, the unusual. Our society seeks to banish, often not consciously, those persons and practices that will not submit to laws of supply and demand, efficiency, and regularization.

It is all too easy to exist in an atmosphere of supposed free speech and yet bring such pressures upon the individual that he is afraid to speak openly. . . . There was a time in the American world when Thoreau's advice to "catalogue stars, those thoughts whose orbits are as

---

[13]Isaac B. Singer, *Gimpel the Fool and Other Stories* (New York: Fawcett Crest, 1980) 104.

[14]Eiseley, *The Night Country,* 212-13.

rarely calculated as comets" could be set down without undergoing the scrutiny of twenty editors or publisher's readers.[15]

Certainly we have not improved our writing, our wisdom, or our scholarship. If the humanist—whether physicist, biologist, historian, or religion professor—does not give word to the "open-ended and nov-elty-producing aspect" of nature, who else is there to tell the truth? Perhaps the question of when and what to write resolves itself finally into the question, for whom is it that we write?

"Do you know why I don't publish anything?" asked Menahem-Mendl of Kotzk:

> *I'll tell you why. Who would read me? Not the scientist, not the scholars; they know more than I do. To wish to read me, a man would have to feel that he knows less than I. Who might that be? A poor villager who works hard all week. When would he have the time to open a book? On Shab-bat. When, at what time? Not on Friday night; he would be too tired. Sat-urday morning? Reserved for services. Following which, he comes home at midday, enjoys his meal, rushes through the customary songs and goes to lie down on his sofa, at peace with himself. Finally, he has a chance to glance at a book. He takes mine; he opens it. But he has eaten too much; he feels heavy. He gets drowsier by the minute; he falls asleep, and here is my volume falling from his hands. And is it for him—for that—that I should publish a book?[16]*

Of course, somebody must read the book. And in a day when "the making of many books" has reached monumental proportions, it is often difficult to know whether there will be a reader to make our writ-ing worthy of effort. Readership in the days of proliferation is deter-mined by the guild of referees and by the promotional work of a publisher with a substantial advertising budget. This is not to say that some books are not read because of their value or because of the cu-riosity they arouse. Menahem-Mendl is probably not correct in saying that a person would not likely read his book unless he felt he knew less than the author. One does not have to know less in order to learn.

---

[15]Ibid., 213.

[16]Elie Wiesel, *Souls on Fire* (New York: Vintage Books, 1972) 232.

Nevertheless, the question—for whom shall a book be written?—is important.

Menaham-Mendl might have considered writing for the truth he had discovered, however humbled he may have felt in the face of its incompleteness, its shortcomings. If it is true, as Eiseley tells us, that writing is the key to experiment and memory, the key to our consciousness of otherness, then we must always be willing to risk incompetence and a lack of readership. The writer is an agent of truth. He writes for the sake of truth, for the sake of words, for the sake of what he has contemplated of the nature of things as they really are in their otherness.

> Only the poet who writes speaks his message across the millennia to other hearts. Only in writing can the cry from the great cross on Golgotha still be heard in the minds of men. The thinker of perceptive insight, even if we allow him for the moment to be a porpoise rather than a man, has only his individual glimpse of the universe until such time as he can impose that insight upon unnumbered generations. In centuries of pondering, man has come upon but one answer to this problem: speech translated into writing that passes beyond human mortality.[17]

We write for the truth, for ourselves in our otherness, and for the sake of speech itself. Without writing, the words that call things into being will have a limited effect. Proper use of words creates beauty, meaning, and relations of affection and compassion. Words may also be used in purely functional ways to perpetuate the ongoingness of civilization's synthetic necessities. We live in an age that has devised ways of recording words and keeping them, an age of computers and tapes. It is tempting to assume that writing is no longer essential to our continuing humanity. But writing keeps us in touch with our origins. It allows us greater deliberation and artistry than speech by itself. It touches more profound depths of our concern for beauty and meaning. The play of words on a page is akin to the arrangements of their sounds in our hearing. Writing is the proper vehicle for the contemplative scholar. Writing enables the scholar to describe and to analyze the findings of contemplation with greater adequacy than

---

[17]Eiseley, *The Star Thrower*, 41-42.

unwritten speech. Writing itself is a mode of contemplation, a way of probing the path of discovery. It is in the act of writing that many scholars learn what it is that has been agitating their minds and imaginations, and forcing the authors into their work.

We should write for whomever is interested in the act of creation. Those who know what contemplation is, what writing is, will be drawn to a work that has been obedient to the need to create. There are books that I read because the convention demands it of me. Often they tell me very little about the wonders of human speech as it seeks to produce beauty and communicate the truth of things as they really are. I am aware that I must find in those books what the author did not care to tell me; there may be something of which the author was unaware. I must find the creative truth that lies beneath the surface of a document that was meant to serve a functional end or sought to "apply a method"—a document that could be condensed into a three-page report. Frequently I will find that concealed creativity beneath the report and the book will be redeemed—I will remember its moment of truth.

After you write you must be able to live with what you have done. And that is not easy if you have made of it too much of a ziggurat, a tower of Babel. Then you have forgotten that your writing is part of the working of contemplation, part of the human act of putting speech onto paper in order to tell the truth that you are seeing. From time to time all of us probably feel a certain revulsion at what we have done in this making of many books. However, if we have written because we had little choice, because our spirits demanded it of us, not because the convention or the academic tenure committee required it, then we should be able to live with the results.

Index

MUP *The Contemplation of Otherness*

Designed by Alesa Jones

Composition by MUP Composition Department

Production specifications:
    text paper—60-pound Warren's Olde Style
    endpapers—Multicolor Antique Scarlet
    covers—(on .088 boards) Joanna Kennett #67350
    dust jacket—100-pound enamel. Printed 2 colors,
        PMS 201 (deep red) and PMS 468 (tan), and varnished.

Printing (offset lithography) by Omnipress of Macon, Inc., Macon, Georgia

Binding by John H. Dekker and Sons, Inc., Grand Rapids, Michigan